CALLIMACHUS

CALLIMACHUS

Hymns, Epigrams, Select Fragments

Translated, with an Introduction and Notes,
by Stanley Lombardo and Diane Rayor

With a Foreword by D. S. Carne-Ross

THE JOHNS HOPKINS UNIVERSITY PRESS
BALTIMORE AND LONDON

Originally published in hardcover and paperback, 1988
Second printing, paperback, 1990

The Johns Hopkins University Press
701 West 40th Street
Baltimore, Maryland 21211
The Johns Hopkins Press Ltd., London

LIBRARY OF CONGRESS CATALOGING-IN-PUBLICATION DATA
Callimachus.
Callimachus : hymns, epigrams, select fragments.
Bibliography: p.
1. Callimachus—Translations, English.   I. Lombardo, Stanley, 1943–
II. Rayor, Diane J.   III. Title.
PA3945.E5   1988   881'.01   87-45479
ISBN 0-8018-3280-2 (alk. paper)
ISBN 0-8018-3281-0 (pbk. : alk. paper)

*The paper used in this publication meets the minimum requirements of American
National Standard for Information Sciences—Permanence of Paper for Printed
Library Materials, ANSI Z39.48-1984.*

For Douglass Parker
πατὴρ τοῦ λόγου

CONTENTS

FOREWORD

Poet, scholar, librarian, spokesman for the new poetry of Hellenistic
Greece, Callimachus now makes his poetic debut in this persuasive
translation by Stanley Lombardo and Diane Rayor. They think it
"something of a scandal" that he has had to wait so long for a modern
voice. Perhaps the delay is not so much scandalous as surprising – surprising that he failed to attract his translator earlier in the century, in
the formative days of Modernism when poetry was required to be hard
and witty and allusive, nourished by a good deal of literature. For
Callimachus – the Callimachus certainly of Lombardo and Rayor – is
in many ways a Modernist, a poet who has studied Pound's *Homage* to
good purpose, a radical traditionalist who would understand what
Auden had in mind when he said that "if we talk of tradition today . . .
we mean a consciousness of the whole of the past in the present."

A later Greek poet described Callimachus's work as "full of astringent honey." One may wonder about the honey – the poise and concin-
nity of his versification? – but "astringent" is clearly the right word.
For Callimachus's is a dry poetry, a poetry of the surface, as Eliot said
of Jonson, hinting at no resonant or beguiling deeps. In the hymns to
the gods, for instance, the most substantial block of his work left to
us, we should not look for much in the way of religious emotion or experience. In contrast to the Homeric hymns, where the poet stands
face to face with the myths or rites he relates, here the matter is very
deliberately distanced. "A poet's fictions should at least be plausible,"
Callimachus remarks at one point. These are poems *about* religious
experience, literary poems in which, to quote a recent critic, we see
the author "facing the question of how a learned modern poet could
draw on the riches of Homeric poetry to create a new idiom."

Dry, astringent, yes, but not or not always cold or detached, witness the beautiful verses he wrote on the death of his friend, the poet

Herakleitos (the first of the epigrams*). There are passages in the hymns that we may call religious, in the Greek sense, notably the description of how one sultry noontide, the dangerous hour when the *daemonium meridianum* is at large, the luckless Tiresias stumbled on Athena bathing. And there is pathos in his mother's grief for the blindness inflicted on her son, penalty for having seen what man must not see. We think of Callimachus as primarily a city poet, but he has an eye for the natural world, "the silverslipping streams" of the river Akheloös, "black-pebbled Anauros." He has moments, flashes, of vision, sometimes unexpectedly tender — an altar, for instance: "the spring wind flowers it with dew."

Lombardo and Rayor have played fair with their text, making it new without trying for a meretriciously contemporary note. Often they keep as close to the original as anyone aspiring to turn foreign verse into English verse need do. When called on, their translation does what any fine translation must, claiming a somewhat greater liberty to meet the challenge of verbal or emotional complexity. In the Hymn to Apollo, Callimachus describes the rock formation traditionally held to be the transformed figure of Niobe mourning for her slaughtered children. He calls the rock *dieros*, meaning both "wet" and "living," a marble rock that was once a living woman and is still wet with her tears. "A marbled mass of tears formed to a woman's moan," Lombardo and Rayor write, possibly improving on the Greek.

And there is something else that Callimachus requires of his translator. Whether or not he employs the sophisticated verbal mode that Pound called logopoeia (Pound detected it in Propertius, who was influenced by the Alexandrian master), one often senses *behind* his words something that a literal version could hardly suggest, an attitude *to* the matter in hand which may be more important than the matter itself. In the Apollo hymn, he tells us that the god was only four years old when he built the famous horned altar on Delos. Exclamation mark! "Apollo's first project in urban design," Lombardo and Rayor add. In a similar vein a few lines later, where the god is invoked by his various cult names (some of them quite recherché), Callimachus writes, simply enough, "O Apollo, many call you Boëdrómios," and so forth. This becomes "O bright Apollo / indexed under

*A Greek "epigram" is simply a short poem or lyric and is seldom what we mean by epigrammatic.

Boëdrómios." That is, the translators have found or thought they found not in but behind the words the poet's ironic amusement at his own laborious researches into Greek religious nomenclature.

Intrusive glosses of this sort, were they pervasive, would be distracting. Used sparingly, as they are here, they give us what a straight rendering could not, and what an insensitive reading of the original easily misses, the very individual tone of voice of this poet, neither minor nor quite major but undeniably interesting. Having found his translators, may Callimachus now find the public he deserves.

D. S. Carne-Ross

INTRODUCTION

> Shades of Callimachus, Coan ghosts of Philetas,
> It is in your groves I would walk.
>
> —Ezra Pound, *Homage to Sextus Propertius*

Pound's translation of the opening lines of Propertius's elegy III.1 reminds us that Callimachus was once a name to conjure with. Although two and a half centuries separated Callimachus (fl. 270 B.C.E.) and Propertius (fl. 30 B.C.E.), the Roman poet was not archaizing: Callimachus had created a sense of style and a critical stance that left a decisive mark on Hellenistic and Roman poetry. A Poundian figure who summed up the possibilities of a new era's response to an old and rich poetic tradition, he is of more than a little interest to our own age. That his work has not until now been translated into our own poetic idiom is something of a scandal.

What do we know of him? The entry in the *Suda*, a Byzantine encyclopedia, reads in part:

> Callimachus, son of Battos and Mesatma, of Kyrênê, a man of letters . . . assiduous enough to have written poems in every meter and a great number of prose works beside, 800 volumes in all. He lived during the reign of Ptolemy Philadelphos [285–247 B.C.E.]. Before his introduction to that king he taught grammar in Eleusis, a suburb of Alexandria. He survived to the time of Ptolemy Euergetes [Philadelphos's successor].

We can add to this Callimachus's own claim that he was descended from Battos, the semimythical founder of Kyrene (an old Greek colony in North Africa). We learn from another source (a scholium in a manuscript of Plautus) that Callimachus held a royal appointment in the great Library of Alexandria. Whether he was ever head librarian is a disputed point—he probably never was—but we do know that he

produced a catalogue, the *Pinakes,* of the library's holdings. His celebrated maxim *"Mega biblion, mega kakon"* ("Big book, big bother") is
probably to be understood in the context of his work as a librarian, but
is in accord with his aesthetic canons as well. He was something of a
court poet (Ptolemy Philadelphos was a patron of the arts and of learning), but we do not really know what being a court poet entailed.
There is little enough adulation in Callimachus's poetry—a few passages in the hymns, *The Lock of Berenike,* and one epigram to Berenike are about the only examples we have—and what adulation there
is is handled so gracefully and humorously as to be inoffensive even to
our egalitarian sensibilities.

More interesting than Callimachus's relationship to Alexandrian
royalty is the literary quarrel he is reported to have had with his
fellow poet Apollonios of Rhodes and with Rhodian critics. Once
again the evidence is slight and controversial. Ancient biographies of
Apollonios tell us that he was originally Callimachus's student, published a first edition of his epic poem the *Argonautika* at Alexandria,
moved to Rhodes when the poem was poorly received, completed a
revised, more successful version of his *Argonautika* in Rhodes, and
later returned to Alexandria, where he became head of the library.
When he died he was buried with Callimachus. The biographies do
not mention any bad feeling between the two poet-scholars, the only
direct evidence for a quarrel being a few scanty references connecting
Callimachus's *Ibis,* an invective poem, with Apollonios, and an epigram perhaps attributable to Apollonios deriding Callimachus and his
poem the *Aetia.* Nothing is left of the *Ibis,* but we do have Callimachus's Prologue to the *Aetia* an attack on his Rhodian critics:

> The malignant gnomes who write reviews in Rhodes
>   are muttering about my poetry again—
> tone-deaf ignoramuses out of touch with the Muse—
> because I have not consummated a continuous epic
>   of thousands of lines on heroes and lords
> but turn out minor texts as if I were a child
>   although my decades of years are substantial.
> To which brood of cyrrhotic adepts
>   I, Callímachus, thus:

A scholium on this passage lists the names of the Rhodian critics in
question; Apollonios is not among them. On the other hand, the

Argonautika is the sort of long, continuous poem Callimachus rejects here and condemns in some detail in the rest of the passage (see below and the translation and notes). We cannot hope to settle the biographical question involved here. The aesthetic one is worth a closer look, and it requires a broad historical and literary perspective.

With the death of Alexander, in 323 B.C.E., the time of Greek cultural expansion ended. The composition of the *Iliad* was some four hundred years in the past, Sappho's work slightly less than three hundred. By the middle of the fifth century Simonides and Aeschylos were dead and Pindar was to die in a few years. Euripides died in 406, Sophocles within months; *The Frogs* of Aristophanes mourns them both, and foretells the death of tragedy. By 380 Aristophanes too was dead. On campaign against the Persians, Alexander kept the text of Homer, hand-corrected by Aristotle, under his pillow, a new Achilles to wreak havoc in Asia, and the last of the heroes. When Callimachus began to write early in the next century he stood in the wake of extraordinary, irreproducible accomplishment. He would have appreciated Yeats's lines:

> Though the great song return no more
> There's keen delight in what we have:
> The rattle of pebbles on the shore
> Under the receding wave.
> — *The Nineteenth Century and After*

The dilemma had already been posed by Aristophanes' contemporary Choerilos of Samos:

> Blessed were the poets in the old days
> When the field was still wide open. The arts
> Are all fenced in now, the field parceled out,
> And we, the latecomers, scratched from the race
> No room to bring up a new-yoked chariot.

By the time Callimachus began to write, the situation no longer involved the sulky anxiety of Choerilos. Some new beginnings had been made: Menander's New Comedy in Athens, Herondas's *Mimiambi* with its realistic sketches of Alexandrian lowlife, Theocritos's invention of pastoral, Aratos's revival of didactic poetry, a renewal of interest in epigram. But these various movements, while presenting new possibilities, also remind us of the increased distance between a poet of Callimachus's period and the past's integral traditions. And, more significantly for any poet who was to take those traditions into account, the shape of the world—that is, the notional shape of the world—had changed.

Greek intellectual life had never been entirely parochial, but Alexander's conquests opened up for it an unprecedented physical scope. The enormous financial resources of the Persian Empire came under control of the new Greek monarchies. Greek cultural hegemony was unbroken from the Euphrates to the central Mediterranean, with outposts further east and west. World affairs became largely a Greek, internal matter, and would remain so until the advent of Roman power. Within the universal *oikúmenê*, the "inhabited space" crowded with activity and information, the cultural task was that of assimilation and rationalization. Local literary and religious traditions melted into a wider continuum, just as the discrete Greek dialects yielded to *koinê*, the "common speech." The common Greek past was assembled in the libraries of Pergamum, Antioch, and above all Alexandria to be annotated and digested by a new generation of scholars. The Hellenistic Age was a time of intense scientific and mathematical development (Euclid and Archimedes were Hellenistic men) and of engineering and rational city planning. It was also a time of systematic philosophies, the schools of Plato and Aristotle, Stoicism and Epicureanism. Hellenistic man knew a great deal and wielded great power to accommodate the uncanny to the familiar. On the world map there was no *terra incognita*; in the plenum of knowledge there was no gap that could not be filled. An open field had been replaced by a much larger but essentially closed field.

As a scholar, Callimachus made significant contributions to the great Hellenistic project of collecting, arranging, and classifying the whole of Greek culture. We have the titles of numerous prose works (none of which survive) that entailed cataloguing and categorization: *Customs of Foreign Peoples, On Winds, Names of Months According to Peoples and Cities, On the Rivers of the World, On the Founding of Islands and Cities and Changes of Names, Ethnically Varying Names,* and *Curiosities Collected All Over the World According to Place.* And there was the *Pinakes,* which rationalized literary history, organizing it formally by author and genre. However the *Pinakes* was actually used in the library, it completed the enterprise the library was in fact engaged in: it made all past literature effectively contemporaneous, arranging it there on the shelves (or their equivalent) in a formal system, part of which was the establishment of a standard canon of authors and works—the creation, in fact, of classic texts.

This enterprise created the possibility of a new relation between the poet and past literary texts, which now become formal objects subject to the organizing, discriminating, selective eye of the writer. As a poet, Callimachus responded to the challenge of the tradition he helped formulate with omnivorous virtuosity and refined selectivity. He composed extensively in most if not all of the genres of Greek poetry, but he chose his own lines of development.

Perhaps a tenth, no more, of his poetry survives: six hymns (his only work to survive in an independent manuscript tradition), sixty-four epigrams, and fragments of elegiac, narrative, lyric, and satiric verse. Some of the fragments can be supplemented by informed conjecture and comparison with versions done by Roman poets; the rest is in tatters. No other Greek poet has demonstrated such range; no other Greek poet was so manifestly concerned with matters of style, taste, and technical acumen. Beside the lines already quoted from the Prologue to the *Aetia* we may set an epigram Callimachus composed on Aratos's *Phaenomena* (a didactic poem on constellations and weather signs) as another stylistic manifesto:

> Arátos of Soloi models his verse
> On Hesiod's best, and refuses to write
> The Ultimate Epic. We praise these terse,
> Subtle tokens of long effort at night.

Callimachus praises Aratos because (1) he consciously, but selectively, models his verse on an ancient author; (2) he chooses as his model not Homer—he does not try to write heroic epic—but Hesiod, a poet with a sensible poetic economy; (3) his style is terse and subtle—the adjective in Greek is *lepton*, a term Aratos had encoded in his text (*Ph.* 783–87) as an acrostic in a passage describing the crescent moon as slight, subtle, fine, attenuated; (4) his writing reflects a certain self-consciousness, for he presents signs and tokens (*semata*) and invites us to read his poem about signs reflectively, even semiotically; (5) his poem is studied, polished, the result of long effort, a virtuoso piece. Callimachus saw in Aratos's *Phaenomena* a model of what poetry could be in the postheroic, posttragic age.

Didactic epos was one of the few genres Callimachus did not

attempt, which is surprising when we think of his prose catalogues; perhaps he felt Aratos had already filled that niche. His own choices for epos (an extensive genre term comprising anything in dactylic hexameter) were the narrative hymn, modeled on the Homeric hymns (which Alexandrian scholarship had determined, probably correctly, were not by Homer) and the epyllion. The epyllion ("miniature epic") was a new direction in Alexandrian poetry. Callimachus's *Hekale*, of which only fragments are left, was one of the prototypes of the form, which is best illustrated by Catullus's *Wedding of Peleus and Thetis* and Vergil's *Ciris*. The narrative in an epyllion shunts off the heroic action to the fringes and in what begins as a digression concentrates in loving detail upon a minor episode or character. Hekale, an old woman who entertained Theseus en route to his bout with the Bull of Marathon, displaces the hero in Callimachus's epyllion. Callimachus probably discovered her while studying local Athenian lore.

Callimachus's great achievement in narrative verse, the *Aetia* (the title means "causes" or "origins"), was in the elegiac rather than the epic tradition. It was a long poem (several thousand lines) composed of short pieces of varying length linked together by the motif suggested by the title, an etiological inquisitiveness into cultural practices and legend. Callimachus is at his best here, adroitly combining learned curiosity, playfulness, psychological interest and a crisp, objective style. The two pieces best represented, besides the Prologue, are the *Lock of Berenike* and *Akontios and Kydippe*. The former, translated by Catullus (and reconstructured here largely on the basis of that translation), represents a type of narrative in the *Aetia* that inspired Ovid's *Metamorphoses*. *Akontios and Kydippe* is a fair sample of Callimachus as a love elegist.

Several other passages from the poems add depth to our understanding of Callimachus's literary program. Here is the conclusion to the *Hymn to Apollo:*

And Envy whispered in Apollo's ear:
"I am charmed by the poet who swells like the sea."
But Apollo put foot to Envy and said:
"The river Euphrates has a powerful current
but the water is muddy and filled with refuse.
The Cult of the Bees brings water to Deo

but their slender libations are unsullied and pure,
the trickling dew from a holy spring's height."

Well done, my Lord, and serve my Critics the same.

Envy suggests that "the sea" is the model of excellence in poetry.
Apollo does not deny this, but contrasts the muddiness of the great
Euphrates with the purity of droplets from a mountain spring. The sea
is a metaphor for Homer, whose poems are expansive, pure (the
Greeks thought of the sea as essentially pure), and the source of all
later poetry (as the sea was thought to be the source of all other
waters). The Euphrates represents later traditional epic poetry, which
in its long course has become murky and stale. Apollo proposes a
"slender libation" (the word again is *lepton*) such as the Bees, priestesses of Demeter, bring to their goddess. Apollo offers similar counsel
in the *Aetia* Prologue:

When I first put a tablet on my knees, the Wolf-God
	Apollo appeared and said:
"Fatten your animal for sacrifice, poet,
	but keep your Muse slender."
And
	"follow trails unrutted by wagons,
don't drive your chariot down public highways,
	but keep to the back roads though the going is narrow.
We are poets for those who love
	the cricket's high chirping, not the noise of the jackass."

Here is a poet who values most what is most likely to escape ordinary
notice, the small and the recondite, the nuances of peripheral vision,
and the fine cords of attention that try to keep them in place. Charac-
teristically his verse proceeds by indirection and ellipsis. Everywhere
the reader must be alert to the voice of what seems to be a peremptory
literary personality, ironic, self-assured—more than a little like Ben
Jonson or Ezra Pound in this—and, like them, inclined to strike poses.
The Prologue continues:

A long-eared bray for others, for me delicate wings,
	dewsip in old age, and bright air for food,
mortality dropping from me like Sicily shifting

its triangular mass from Enkélados's chest.
No nemesis here:
>the Muses do not desert the gray heads
of those on whose childhood
>>their glance once brightened.

This is not poetry for everyone's taste, nor is it meant to be. Without the most prodigious capacity for learning, patience, and complex emotional discrimination, the general reader is apt to be dismissed with contempt, along with everything else that smacks of the mass market:

>I hate the poems in the Epic Cycle, I don't like highways
>>that are heavily traveled, I despise
>a promiscuous lover, and I don't drink from public fountains:
>>Everything public disgusts me. And yes, Lysánias,
>you are handsome as handsome, but before I can even say it,
>>back comes the echo: "Some other man has him."

There is fun in this snobbery for some. Yet, beyond the testy exclusivity, there is a real poet in Callimachus and a real poet's concern for practiced, responsible speech. No bardic frenzy here: Callimachus is one of the most disciplined poets in the ancient world. He has limited the scale of his work to the "minor texts" his critics complain of only to call the limitation to account for the sake of a meticulously realized texture. The diction is true, the verse delicately cadenced, its sonorities balanced and under tight control. In the Greek text of the epigram quoted above, the presence of Echo is justified in part by an assonantal correspondence between the description of Lysanias, *naikhi kalos kalos,* and the last words of the poem, *allos ekhei* (a correspondence preserved in the translation by "handsome as handsome" and "some other man has him"). Everywhere in the poems the rhythm of argument, the flow of details—and with them our attention—are modulated with unerring accuracy; the nuance, though rich and almost unimaginably complex, is still subtle and precisely governed. For the care lavished on his linguistic surface, Callimachus has been called a poet's poet, bookish, and a technician; these things are true, but he is also a poet of the profoundest tact—not timidity, tact—which means nothing more or less than that he gives each thing its due, scrupulously, tenderly weighing and composing, because so much depends on getting it right. This is why the great generation of Roman poets—Vergil, Propertius, Catullus, Ovid—grappled with a powerful fascination for his work: they were drawn to him because he was a poet of a way of writing. The poetry seldom glares, it glances. The particular things of the world do not glare back, falsely naked, but rather peer out from a nest of considered contextual detail, which for Callimachus is their true home, or at least the only home we can talk about and know. Verse like this is rare, but the things of the world and the language that tries to comprehend them deserve no less respect.

The most obvious manifestation of Callimachus's regard for the particular is the crowd of proper names everywhere in his poetry. At first this seems to be simply the poetic reflex of the prose cataloguer. In a fragment of uncertain location Callimachus vows, "I sing nothing untestified"; and he declares in the *Hymn to Artemis:* "Your catalogue will be my song." In the opening lines of Hymn I the poet is playfully at the mercy of the scholar:

Eternal Lord, eternally great, mythic scourge
of the Sons of Earth, lawgiver to the Sons of Heaven,
Diktaîan, Lykaîan—how praise the mountain-born god?
       Disputed nativity
divides the mind in doubt.
          Cretan hills of Ida, Zeus?
Arkádia?
Of these claimants, which has lied, Father?

But names are not confined to any particular rhetorical situation. They are everywhere: names of mountains, islands, rivers, cities, of individual men and women, nations, and gods with their regional titles and cult epithets, names present and past—a universe of names. Many are strange and deliberately so (even the best commentators sometimes throw up their hands), as if names had a quality of their own, independent of the things they signify. Other are familiar, even after all these years, as if to reassure us of the stability of the world and its accessibility to language. Names can call notice to the presence of things with a clamor:

Aetna cried aloud,
Sicily shouted—
seat of Sikanians—

her neighbor Italy
screamed, and Corsica
rumbled and roared.

Even when things are more fugitive, there is still a scrupulous precision in the use of names:

Arkádia dodged her
and the holy hill Parthénion
 ran away, and old Pheneîos Town
the whole land of Pelops up to the Isthmos
save Síkyon and Argos (which Leto avoided
since these lands were Hera's).
 Aónia too fled,
Dirke and Stróphia, Theban rivers, tumbled after,
hand in hand with their black-pebbled father.

Names play a role in an elaborate rhetoric of specificity. At the end of the twenty-eighth epigram names focus our attention like a lens on the unaccountable elegance of the particular:

But do thou, Goddess, give grace
 To the daughter of Kleînias.
She is intelligent and does everything well,
 And she comes from Aiólian Smyrna.

Or names can occasion other names, all but burying the thing-in-itself in a heap of librarian's glosses, as in the second hymn, where the strategy of a translation is to capture the spirit of the passage with a pointed anachronism:

O bright Apollo,
 indexed under Boëdrómios,
 under Klários,
 polynomial,
I and my fathers call you Karneîos:
 Sparta first   you founded,
 then Thera   six generations from Oedipus,
 Kyrénê third,   leading bulls to Asbýstia
 to fall at your festival.

Names allow Callimachus to chart the meanderings of history, and some of his poems recall the origin of specific names: Samos, Lipara, the river Neda, the "Umbilical Plain" on Crete, or the cliff the Kydonians call "Net Mountain." In the fourth hymn an island wanders uncertainly over the sea until, by a miracle, it is fixed in place and wins the name we know, Delos, the "Clear Island." In other poems, all that is left of the past is its names, most commonly among the sepulchral epigrams, where it is also most natural. A tombstone gives name to a once-living body, definitively elusive, locus now only of memory and a sense of loss. The second epigram memorializes the pathos of a nexus of names inscribed on a stone:

"Timónoê."
              Who are you, lady,
      besides a name on a tombstone
determined by other names:
                                Timótheos,
your father, and Methýmna,
      your city, and your husband,
Euthýmenes,
            widowed and grieving.

In the fourth epigram the name of the dead has disappeared:

Shipwrecked stranger, Leóntikhos found your
Anonymous corpse and gave you burial
On the seabeach here. His tears, though, were for
His own mortality. Restless sailor,
He beats over the sea like a flashing gull.

The focus moves at midpoem to the restless, shifting, self-conscious author of the monument, who nevertheless acts with perfect propriety and exits deftly with haunting grace. This epigram takes its place among Callimachus's other icons for his poetic activity.

In a poem entitled *To the Reader*, the epigrammatist J. V. Cunningham has written what might almost serve as Callimachus's epitaph:

Time will assuage.
Time's verses bury

Margin and page
In commentary.

For gloss demands
A gloss annexed
Till busy hands
Blot out the text,

And all's coherent.
Search in this gloss
No text inherent.
The text was loss.

The gain is gloss.

Callimachus's text has in modern times been the province solely of scholarly commentators. Callimachus invites, demands commentary, and much that has been done is enlightening (see the notes to the individual poems for bibliographical references). But his text also demands to be restored to the poetry-reading public, and to the poets. That is the province of translation and the purpose of this translation. We have aimed at a mean between a literal prose crib and free imitation, producing poetry out of poetry by whatever tactics suggested themselves, as long as we followed the contours and spirit of Callimachus's verse. Our intention as translators has been (as Diane Rayor aptly puts it) to produce English poetry that affects the reader in the way Callimachus's Greek poetry has affected us.

Our own verse forms range from traditional rhymed quatrains in some of the epigrams to the occasional use of free broken lines in the hymns. Callimachus's frequent, often abrupt digressions and shifts in tone are generally marked in the translation by changes in the metrical format, both visual and aural. In the narrative poems (including the hymns) our workhorse is a line with from four to six principal beats, a weak caesura (midline break), and more syllables unstressed than stressed. The opening lines of Hymn IV illustrate some of the permutations of the four-beat version of the line:

When will my sóul   sing holy Délos,
mágical Délos,   bifth-ísle of Apóllo?
All of the Cýcladês   are núminous íslands,
but Délos líes   like a póem in the séa.

Line endings such as "sing holy Delos," "isle of Apollo," and "numinous islands" happen to be accentual approximations of the last two feet — dactyl-trochee or dactyl-spondee — of the Greek quantitative dactylic hexameter, the meter in the hymns. But that is only a serendipitous echo and not a consistent feature of the translation or even one that we sought. Classical Greek meters do not naturalize well into English. The longer, six-beat line is built of one and a half of the four-beat lines, so that two of the longer lines equal three of the shorter:

Etérnal Lórd,   etérnally gréat,   mýthic scoúrge
of the Sóns of Eárth,   lawǵíver   to the Sóns of Heáven

The real guiding principle and test of the translation's verse, however, is the ear; the verse here, like Callimachus's own, is designed to be read out loud. As an aid to the reader, the following diacritical marks have been added to proper names in the translations: the umlaut indicates that two adjacent vowels do not form a diphthong; the circumflex is used over accented diphthongs and final long e; otherwise, the acute accent is used to mark the word accent. The advantage of using lines of varying length and free verse to translate Callimachus's comparatively regular dactylic verse is that, as indicated above, it brings metrical resources to bear on the problem of establishing the rhetorical shape of the poem, on both a large and a small scale. It also frees the translator's diction, making more words available at any one point in the attempt to reproduce the Callimachean/Poundian "exact treatment of the thing."

The writing of this book was partially funded by a grant from the University of Kansas General Research Fund.

I would like to thank my co-translator, Diane Rayor, who brought a dormant project back to life when she joined me in the work; Jack Winkler for his acute reading of an earlier version of this translation; and William Levitan for invaluable formative criticism at every stage of the work.

STANLEY LOMBARDO
UNIVERSITY OF KANSAS

HYMNS

Hymn I: To Zeus

What song but of Zeus for the God's libations?
Eternal Lord, eternally great, mythic scourge
of the Sons of Earth, lawgiver to the Sons of Heaven,
Diktaîan, Lykaîan—how praise the mountain-born god?
      Disputed nativity   5
divides the mind in doubt.
      Cretan hills of Ida, Zeus?
Arkádia?
Of these claimants, which has lied, Father?
"Cretans are always liars."   10
And your Cretan-built tomb, my Lord,
will never hold your immortal essence.

On Parrhásia, Rheîa bore you, in Arkádia, where
the mountain is shaded with thickest thornbush.
That is holy ground now. No creeping thing,   15
no woman in labor seeks Eileithyîa in that
immemorial Apidanian birthbed of Rheîa.
There mother deposited you from the laps and folds
of her body divine, and sought running water
to cleanse herself after birth's defilement   20
and to wash your skin, Zeus.

     But mighty Ladon
   was not a flow yet, nor Eurymánthos
     whitest of rivers,
  and all of Arkádia was a waterless parch   25
which hereafter was called well-watered and -streamed.
At the moment when Rheîa slackened her clothes
     old hollow oaks
   shaded Iaon's moist surge,
    Melas was creaking with traffic of wagons,   30
  and serpents coiled and swarmed in their lairs
     above Karneîon's wetness,
     and a man on foot
  might pass above Krathis and pebbled Metópê,

thirsty for all of the water beneath him.   35
And Lady Rheîa, in the grip of distress, said:

"Earth, dear, deliver—your birth pains are easy!"

Poised in her speech with great arm held high,
the goddess struck: staff to the mountains and water asunder
poured from the rift. In this, O my Lord,   40
she brightened your flesh, and swaddled and gave you
to Neda, your escort to Crete and a secret upbringing,
Neda, the eldest of those midwifing nymphs
in that earliest birth after Phílyra and Styx.
No idle grace repaid this service: 45
the goddess named that river Neda.
    Full in its course
    it passes close
    to the Kaukonian city
    known as   50
    Lepreîon,
    then
    mingles with Nereus,
    river with sea,
    its ancient waters   55
    drunk by Arkadians
    the Sons of the Bear.

Carrying you to Knossos
the nymph left Thenai,
and at that point, Zeus-Father,   60
near Thenai-by-Knossos,
your navel, Divine One,
dropped to the ground,
on the Umbilical Plain
as the Kydonians still call it.   65

But your godself the hetairae of the Korybants cradled,
the ash-nymphs of Diktê, and Adrestaîa tucked you
in the golden crib, and you sucked butterfat milk
from the goat Amaltheîa, and consumed honeycomb sweets,

spontaneous generation of the Panakrian bee 70
on those hills of Ida known as Panákra.
And the Kurétes orchestrated an armordance round you,
beating shields like cymbals so that Kronos would hear
bombilating weaponry, but not you playing baby.

You were a lovely child, Zeus: well fed, you grew tall, 75
swift adolescence, rapid fuzz to your cheeks.
But your youth was wise: you were a young Perfect Master.
And for this your high kindred, though of the Elder Race,
conceded you the sky as your rightful home.
Old poets lie when the say that the lot 80
assigned triplicate homes to the sons of Kronos.
Who would play dice for Olympos and Hades
except a green novice? The stakes should be equal
for a gamble like this. These were whole worlds apart.

A poet's fiction should at least be plausible. 85

Not the luck of the draw made you shah of the gods
                but Strength in your hands
Force crouched by your throne
                and Power beside it.
And as for your portent you drafted the most 90
magnificent of birds (may he flash on my right)
so also of men you chose the greatest as yours,
not seacaptains, not soldiers, no, not even poets—
these you dismissed to lesser divinities,
other wards for other gods—but reserved for yourself 95
KINGS, rulers of cities,
under whose hands are
landowners,
        oarswingers,
                    spearmongers, 100
                tradesmen
                        and whatnot.

So we say: blacksmiths belong to Hephaîstos,
        mercenaries to Ares,

hunters to Artemis Khiton,   105
        and to Apollo those who strum tunes on a lyre.
But KINGS are from Zeus, and there is nothing more divine
than God's own lords.
                        And so you chose them to sponsor,
gave them cities to guard, and took your position   110
in the high citadels, a monitor of judgments
straight and crooked, to see how they govern.
                        And you lavished wealth
and prosperity on them, on all, but not equally
if we may judge by our monarch,   115
for Ptolemy Philadélphos is preeminent by far.
He accomplishes by dusk what he thinks of at dawn—
the monumental by dusk, the minor in a trice—
while the projects of others drag on for years,
their programs curtailed by your executive order.   120

A Royal Salute to the Son of Kronos most high!
Benefactor and Savior, who could hymn your works?
That poet hasn't been born,
inconceivable poet of the works of Zeus.

A second salute, Father! Dispense goodness and wealth: 125
Wealth without goodness is a worthless increase,
and goodness needs substance.
                        Bless us with both, Zeus.

Hymn II: To Apollo

Vibrations from Apollo's laurel branch
stir tremors through the temple.
       Depart from here, O you sinners,
Phoîbos taps the door with lovely foot.

Don't you see, the Delian 5
              palm tree nodded,
a sudden sweetness, the swan sings in air,
bolts slide from the door, the hinges swing

The god is no longer far.

Young men, prepare for the choral dance. 10
Apollo's epiphanies are not for all:
Magnificent to see the god
              and graceless not to see him;
we shall see you and never be graceless,
O HEKAÉRGOS, your power is from afar. 15

Let the children not hold the lyre silent
or footsteps soundless
              when Phoîbos is present
if they wish to marry and cut gray hair
and the city walls stand on ancient foundations. 20

Now the lyre shell trembles
              and these children charm me.
Be still to hear the song of Apollo, hear
the hush of the sea when the minstrels sing
the lyre and bow of Lykórean Phoîbos 25
   and the wail of Thetis trails off in the sea.
   She keens no more for her dear son Achilles
   when she hears HIÉ PAIÉON HIÉ.
And that mournful rock that stands in Phrygia
a marbled mass of tears formed to a woman's moan 30
aches no more when it hears HIÉ.
Chant the anthem: HIÉ! Reprehensible

to contest the immortals:
    Oppose the gods and oppose my monarch,
    My monarch oppose and Apollo too.   35
But he will honor the chorus that sings to his heart,
For his power is from the right hand of Zeus,
And this chorus will sing for more than one day:
What poet could fail with Phoîbos for theme?
    Golden the tunic and cloak of Apollo,   40
    The lyre, the Lýktian arrow and bow,
    And golden his sandals, an aureate god:
    Assess his wealth from deposits at Pytho.
And he is beautiful, and eternally young.
Cheeks not even shadowed by down, his fragrant hair   45
sheds essence to earth, no pomade for Apollo
but pure Panacea, a distillation
to immunize cities wherever it falls.

And Apollo as patron is unparalleled.
His province includes the archer and poet   50
(the lyre and bow are proper to Phoîbos)
as well as prophets and seers. It is from Phoîbos
physicians have learned deferment of death.

And we call Phoîbos "Pastor" from the time when he tended
mares by Amphrýssos out of love for Admétos.   55
The god burned with desire, and the herd multiplied,
and the flocks of goats became thronged with young
when Apollo cast eye on them as they fed,
and the sheep became pregnant, swollen with milk,
and lambs ingeminated in their mothers' wombs.   60

And men follow Phoîbos when surveying cities,
for Phoîbos is fond of establishing towns,
a foundation deity who in his fourth year
laid out his first walls at Ortygian Delos,
a lovely landscape with an encircling lake.   65
Artemis hunted for Kynthian goats
and Apollo plaited their horns for a shrine
and built the altar's foundations of horn,

with horn framed the altar and surrounded the shrine
with walls of horn, Apollo's first project in urban design.　　70

And Phoîbos told Battos of my city's deep soil:
as a raven he led my people to Libya,
an omen and oath of walls for our kings.
Apollo is ever true to his oaths.

O bright Apollo,　　75
　　indexed under Boëdrómios,
　　　　under Klários,
　　　　polynomial,
I and my fathers call you Karneîos:
　　　　Sparta first　　you founded,　　80
　　　　then Thera　　six generations from Oedipus,
　　　　Kyrénê third,　leading bulls to Asbýstia
　　　　to fall at your festival,
　　　their wet haunches on your pied altar,
　　　but the spring wind flowers it with dew　　85
　　　and in winter the crocus
　　　　　　　　　an eternal flame
to make the god smile
when the soldiers danced with the women of Libya,
golden women with belted warriors　　90
　　　　　　　　　at his Karneian festival,
the Dorians not yet at the stream of Kyrê,
but still in the woods of Azíris,

And showed these dancers to his bride Kyrénê,
she and her lord on the Hill of Myrtles,　　95
where Kyrénê had slain the lion,
bane to the kine of Eurýpylos.
Apollo rejoiced in these dancers
and honored that city, remembering
his passion for the woman,　　100
and no other god is honored more
than Phoîbos Apollo by the sons of Battos.

Hear the refrain from Delphi: PAIÉON HIḖ!

For Apollo descended with golden bow
To the dread goddess serpent that lay at Pytho.   105
To the peoples' cry "Shoot it, Hië!"
He murdered the monster with arrow on arrow.

This god his mother bore for our salvation.

And Envy whispered in Apollo's ear:
"I am charmed by the poet who swells like the sea."   110
But Apollo put foot to Envy and said:
"The river Euphrates has a powerful current
but the water is muddy and filled with refuse.
The Cult of the Bees brings water to Deo
but their slender libations are unsullied and pure,   115
the trickling dew from a holy spring's height."

Well done, my Lord, and serve my Critics the same.

Hymn III: To Artemis

      (not lightly do poets forget her)
we sing

      who amuses herself on mountains
      with archery and hareshoots   5
        and wide circle dances.

When she was still just a slip of a goddess,
she sat on her father's knee and said:
      "I want to be a virgin forever,
Papa, and I want to have as many names   10
as my brother Phoîbos, and please, Papa,
give me a bow and some arrows—please?—
not a big fancy set: the Cýclopês can make me
some slender arrows and a little, curved bow.

"And let me be Light Bringer   15
and wear a tunic with a colored
border down to the knee, loose
for when I go hunting wild game.

"And give me sixty dancing girls,
        daughters of Ocean,   20
   all nine years old
        all little girl seanymphs,
and twenty woodnymphs from Amnísos for maids
to take care of my boots and tend my swift hounds
      when I'm done shooting lynx and stag, and   25

"Give me all the mountains in the world, Papa,
and any old town, I don't care which one:
Artemis will hardly ever go down into town.
I'll live in the mountains, and visit men's cities
only when women, struck with fierce labor pangs,   30
call on my name, for the Moirai ordained

when I was being born, that Artemis be
a helper of women, because mother in bearing
and birthing me had no pain at all: I just
slipped right out of her dear round belly."   35

And with that she stretched out her hands
to her father's beard, but hard as she tried
couldn't reach his whiskers; and he nodded,
laughing and caressing her, and said:

"When goddesses bear me children like this,   40
I hardly mind Hera's jealous anger.
                                        Take,
child, everything you want, and Father
will give you other things even better:

"I will give you thirty citadels, not just one,   45
thirty cities with towers that will know to exalt
Artemis alone, thirty cities to call your own!
And quite a few more to share with other gods, inland
and island, with altars and groves of Artemis in all.

"And you will be Guardian of Harbors and Roads."   50

    No sooner said than done, confirmed
    with an Olympian nod of his head.

The girl walked upon
the white Cretan mountain,
through its thick woods,   55
and on to the Ocean,
picked out her nymphs,
all nine years old,
all still little girls.

    Rejoice, river Kaîratos,   60
    Tethys, rejoice
    for daughters sent to serve
    Leto's own daughter.

And she was off to the Cýclopês on Lípara Isle
(Lípara now, but called Melígunis then),   65
found them standing around the anvils of Hephaîstos
hammering a red-hot mass of iron to fashion
a monumental watering trough for Poseidon's horses.

The nymphs trembled at the sight
of these monsters, rough as Ossan cliffs,   70
one eye beneath each beetling brow
glaring like a four-ply oxhide shield,
trembled at the anvil's thud,
the deafening blast from the bellows,
the Cýclopês' groans.   75

   Aetna cried aloud,
   Sicily shouted—
   seat of Sikanians—
   her neighbor Italy
   screamed, and Corsica   80
   rumbled and roared,

  when they raised hammers high or took sizzling
  bronze from the forge or hammered iron in turn
  striking the anvil with a chorus of grunts.

The Daughters of Ocean didn't dare ignore them,   85
nor look them in the eye, nor unstop their ears,
and no wonder: not even the Blessed Ones' daughters,
well past toddlerhood, can look without shuddering.
When some (not so divine) little girl disobeys,
her mother calls out the Cýclopês on the child,   90
Arges or Steropes, and up from the basement,
smeared with ashes, Hermes comes and plays bogy
to the frightened child, who hides her eyes
with her hands and runs plunging into mother's lap.

But you, Goddess, were only three years old   95
when Leto first took you to Hephaîstos's forge
(he had some presents to give you). Brontês
set you upon his stout knees, and you plucked

shaggy hair out of his chest, tore it right out,
so that even today his sternum is hairless   100
(you would think the monster had a touch of mange).

Nor did you mince words with them now, Goddess:
"Cýclopês, make me a Cretan bow, and a quiver
full of arrows, for I too am a child of Leto,
no less than Apollo. And whatever wild animals   105
I kill in the hunt the Cýclopês may have as meat."

And as you spoke they filled your order.

You were ready in a flash, Goddess,
and off to get whelps for your pack.
Here is the Arkadian tent of Pan,   110
Pan in front butchering lynx from Maînalos
for the bitches to eat, and the grizzled god
gave you:
            two half-white dogs,
            three with hanging ears,   115
            one speckled   (these could pull down lions,
                                seize their throats, and
                                drag them home still alive)
            and seven Spartan bitches
                                (swifter than wind in pursuing   120
                                fawns and wide-eyed hare,
                                keen on the scent of stag,
                                porcupine, and the trace of gazelle).

        And you were gone, dogs running along,
to the foot of the Parrhásian mountain,   125
frisky deer there browsing on the banks
of black-pebbled Anaúros, deer bigger
than bulls, and their horns shone with gold.
Struck with wonder you said to yourself:
"Here is a first catch worthy of Artemis."   130
Leaving the dogs behind, to get the deer
unharmed, you caught four of the five
to pull your chariot: one escaped, hid

by the Keryneîan Hill, guided by Hera
over the Kéladon River, a later labor for Herakles.   135

Artemis, Virgin,
            Killer of Títyos,
in golden armor and belt, you yoked
a golden chariot, bridled deer in gold.

From where did the horned team begin its first run?   140
Thracian Haîmos,
            where Boreas's hurricane
            blows ill frost on the cloakless.

Where did you cut pine for torches,
lit by what flame?   145
            Mysian Olympos.
You breathed into the torches
      the unquenchable light
      of fire distilled from Father's lightning bolts.

How many times, Goddess, did you test   150
your silver bow?
            First you shot an elm,
            an oak, a wild animal;
then you shot into the city of wicked men,
who assault strangers and curse themselves;   155
you pierce them with a cutting anger:

Plague grazes on their cattle, hoarfrost
on their fields; old men cut their hair
mourning for sons, women die giving birth
or escape death with crippled children.   160

But those whom your smile and grace illumine:
their fields flourish with cornears,
their livestock and wealth multiply,
only the very old go to the grave, and strife,
which wastes even well-established houses,   165

avoids the family: wives of brothers and
husband's sisters sit around one table.

                                      Lady,
may my true friends and I be among those,
Queen, and may I always care about song.   170

I will sing
        Leto's wedlock, Apollo,
          and always Artemis:
your labors, dogs, archery, and chariot
that lifts you lightly—behold—on your way   175
to Zeus's heavenly abode.
                    At the door
you hand your weapons to Guileless Hermes,
and Apollo brings in your kill of the day—
at least he used to before Herakles came;   180
now Phoîbos no longer has this labor
because the "Anvil of Tiryns" loiters
by the gates, waiting for you to return
bearing a hunk of fat meat.
                    The gods laugh   185
      at Herakles, especially Hera,
when he lifts from the chariot a great big bull
or a struggling wild boar by its hind foot.
Then he admonishes you,
Goddess, with this cunning speech: 190

"Shoot savage beasts and win praise,
as I have, from mortal men.
Let deer and hare feed in hills—
What harm do deer and hare do?
Pigs ruin fields,   195
ravage gardens, and oxen
are a great evil for men;
shoot them instead."

He spoke and made quick work of the huge beast;
for even though his limbs were deified   200

under a Phrygian oak,
he is still a glutton;
he has the same belly
as when he met Theiodámas plowing.

Freeing them from the yoke, the nymphs of Amnísos   205
rub down your deer and gather
quick-sprouting, three-leaved clover
from Hera's meadow for fodder,
which even the horses of Zeus feed on;
the nymphs fill a golden winevat with water,   210
a delightful drink for deer.

You go in your father's house;
all the gods call you to them
but you sit beside Apollo.

When the nymphs circle you in a dance   215
    near the springs of Egyptian Ínopos
    or your temple at Pitánê, in Límnai,
    —yes, Pitánê too is yours—
    Goddess, or in Alaî Araphénides
    after you left Skythia, denouncing   220
    the custom of the Tauri;

then may my oxen not be under foreign hire,
plowing a fallow field of four acres,
    for they would return to the farmyard
    with weary limbs and neck, even if   225
    they were nine-year-old long-horned
    Stymphaían cattle, who are the best
    at plowing a wide furrow;

because Helios never passes above
    that lovely dance without stopping   230
    his chariot to gaze down:
    lengthening the light of day.

What island, mountain, harbor, and city

now please you most?
                 Which nymph   235
do you love best?
                 Which heroine
is your companion?
                 Tell me, Goddess,
and your catalogue will be my song: 240

Dólikhê Island, the city of Pergê,
Taÿgeton Mountain, the harbor of Eurípos,
please you most.
                 The fawn-slaying nymph of Gortyn,
sharp-shooting Britomartis, you love beyond all   245
others. Frenzied with desire for her, Minos ran
through the mountains of Crete. The nymph hid
now under a shaggy oak, now in a marshy meadow;
Minos wandered nine months over cliffs and crags
in relentless pursuit until, when she was nearly   250
in his grasp, she leapt from the cliff to the sea—
into the saving net of a fishing boat.

So the Kydonians call the nymph
Lady-of-the-Net, and the cliff
where she jumped Net Mountain;   255
there they set up altars and sacrifices,
making garlands of pine or mastich
                 (myrtle they leave untouched,
                 for a myrtle branch
                 caught in the nymph's   260
                 robe when she fled,
                 so she hates myrtle).

Oûpis, my Queen, shining-eyed Light Bringer,
the Cretans even name you after that nymph.

You made Kyrénê, daughter of Hypsios,   265
your companion and gave her two hunting dogs
to win the contest beside the Iolkion tomb.
My Lady, you chose the golden-haired wife

of Képhalos, son of Deiónios, for your hunting
partner and they say you loved the lovely   270
Antikleía like your eyes. Those three first bore
the quick bow and quiver around their shoulders,
the right shoulder and breast always bare.

You lavished praise on swift-footed Atalanta,
boar-killing daughter of Arkadian Iásios;   275
you taught her hunting with dogs and good aim.
The hunters of the Kalydonian boar
couldn't find fault with her; the tokens
of victory, including the tusks of the beast,
went to Arkádia; even though they hate her,   280
centaurs Hylaîos and senseless Rhoîkos in Hades
could hardly criticize Atalanta's archery,
for their wounded flanks were witness;
the Mainalian mountain ridge
    flowed with their blood.   285

Lady of many temples and cities,
hail, Huntress, who resides in Milétos;
you guided Neleus when he led his black ships
from archaic Athens.
            Lady of Khésion, Imbrásia,   290
high throned: Agamemnon dedicated
his ship's rudder to you in your temple;
a sweet charm against storm or deadly calm.
When you bound the winds, the Akhaîan ships
sailed to grieve the cities of the Trojans,   295
maddened over Rhamnusian Helen.

Proîtos built two temples for you,
one to Artemis the Daughter—
because you rescued his daughters
wandering mad through the Azánian   300
Mountains; the other in Lusa
    to Artemis the Mild—
    because you exorcized
the wild spirit from his daughters.

Amazons, lovers of battle, set up   305
a wooden image under an oak
in seaside Éphesos, and Hippo
offered a holy sacrifice to you;
Around the oak they danced you a war dance,
Queen Oûpis, first with shields and then a wide   310
circledance; the shrill pipes joined in lithe song
to keep time
                    (that was before they pierced fawn bones
            for flutes: Athena's evil work for deer)
the echo leapt to Sardis   315
                              and the Berekýnthian song,
their feet clicked quickly, the quivers rattled.

Afterward around that wooden image, wide foundations
were built. Dawn sees nothing richer or more divine;
it easily surpasses Pytho. Lygdámis, violent   320
and psychotic, threatened to raze it; he led an army
of mare-milking Kimmerians numerous as sand,
who live near the Bosporos, passage of Io,
daughter of Ínakhos. Vile King! His transgression meant
that neither he nor his men whose wagons stood   325
in the Kaystrian meadow would return to Skythia;
    your bow always lies before Éphesos.

Lady of Muníkhia, Harbor Watcher,
Lady of Phérai, hail!
May no one dishonor Artemis: 330
    Oíneus dishonored her altars and
    no pretty struggles came to his city;
nor strive in shooting stag or in skillful aim:
    the son of Atreus couldn't boast
    that he paid a small price;   335
nor may anyone woo the virgin:
    neither Otos nor Oríon wooed a good wedding;
nor avoid the annual dance:
    Queen Hippo, not without tears,
    refused to circle the altar.   340

All hail, Goddess, and be gracious to my song.

Hymn IV: To Delos

When will my soul sing holy Delos,
magical Delos, birth-isle of Apollo?
All of the Cýcladês are numinous islands,
but Delos lies like a poem in the sea.
She washed and cradled the archpoet Apollo   5
and first took him for god.
                    The Muses
are piqued if we don't hymn Pimpleía,
and Apollo is angry if we overlook Delos.
The trace of this poem leads us to Delos   10
and its mountain, Kynthos. May Kynthian Apollo
bless my remembrance of his island nurse.

She is a windy rock beaten by waves,
better for gulls than horses, severe,
stuck in the swell that swirls round her sides   15
and flecks her with foam from the Ikarian Sea.
Small-craft fishermen make their homes there.
But the islands freely acknowledge her leader
when they troop out to Ocean and the Titaness Tethys
to hold their convention. In her wake comes Corsica, 20
no island to slight, and lengthy Euboîa,
and lovely Sardinia, and the island where Kypris
first washed ashore and which she protects —
all fortified islands buttressed by towers —
But Delos is sheltered by the strength of Apollo.   25
Walls and stones may fall in the wind
                    when it blows like a Thracian torrent,
but a god stands forever,
                    and you, dear Delos,
are preserved by Apollo's eternal vigilance.   30

Currents of poetry circle around you.
In which shall I lap you?
Which sound fits your mood?
How in the beginning the great god smashed mountains
with the three-tined sword the Telkhínes had made   35

and created the islands by prying them up
and rolling them whole down into the sea?
He rooted them deep to forget the mainland.
But you were not crimped, you floated
free on the waters, and your name of old was   40
Astéria, because you shot like a star
into the abyss to escape Zeus's lust.
Golden Leto was not yet your associate;
you were still Astéria and not yet called Delos.

A sailor would spy you in the Saronic Gulf   45
as he made for old Corinth from the town of blond Tróëzen.
But coming back from Ephýra he could not find you there:
you had slipped into Eurípos, the narrow strait,
and were listening to the current's sharp incantations.
The same day you would turn back from the Sea of Khalkis   50
and swim to Sounion, the Athenian headland,
or to Khios or Parthenia (we now call her Samos)
whose maiden breast is washed in the sea.
And the nymphs of Mykale would entertain you there.
But when you gave your land for Apollo's nativity   55
sailors changed your name and called you Delos,
Clear Island, for you no longer drifted,
but sank your roots in the Aegean Sea.

Nor did you quake when Hera was fuming
at the wombs of women who bore Zeus's children,   60
and Leto especially, who alone carried a child
who would be dearer than Ares. Raging mad
she kept watch from the sky to keep Leto in labor,
and she had on the ground a pair of enforcers:
Ares sat armed on the top of Mount Haîmos   65
and spied on the mainland, his horses uncamped
by the seven caverns of Wind, while Iris streaked
to Ionian Mimas and watched from its peak the isle-dotted sea.
There the two sat, threatening the cities
that Leto approached and barring her reception.   70

     Arkádia dodged her

and the holy hill Parthénion
          ran away, and old Peneîos Town,
the whole land of Pelops up to the Isthmos
save Síkyon and Argos (which Leto avoided   75
since these lands were Hera's).
          Aónia too fled,
Dirkê and Stróphia, Theban rivers, tumbled after,
hand in hand with their black-pebbled father.
Far behind flowed Asópos,   80
his knees heavy with lightning.
          The ashnymph Mélia
          whirled out of the dance,
her cheeks pale as leaves, sighing in terror
for the oak, her sister in earth,   85
when she saw Hélikon shaking her hair.

          But tell me, my Muses,
          is it true that oaks
          and nymphs are coeval?
          The nymphs rejoice   90
          when rain swells the oaks
          and grieve when leaves
          fall from the oaks . . .

But Apollo even in the womb was angry,
threatening Thebes with fated disaster: 95

"Why are you begging
   for your destined doom, Thebes?
Don't force me to be a premature prophet.
My tripod seat is not yet at Pytho,
          the great reptile not dead: 100
that fanged thing still creeps down
from Pleîstos and wraps its coils,
nine times around snowy Parnassos.
Here is an oracle clearer than the laurel's:
          Run as you will!   105
   Soon I will catch you
                    and wash my arrows

in the blood of a libelous Theban woman.
Neither you nor Kithaîron will be my dear nurse;
I am pure and will be cared for only by the pure."   110

He spoke, and Leto turned and went back.
But when the cities of Akhaîa rejected her too,
Hélike (Poseîdon's consort) and Bura,
where the centaur Dexámenos had great cattle stalls,
she backtracked toward Thessaly. Anaúros fled,   115
and great Larísa and the cliffs of Kheiron,
and Peneîos snaked off through the valley of Tempe.
Hera, you did not break down, unmerciful heart,
you did not shed a tear, not even when Leto
stretched out her arms and desperately prayed: 120

"Thessalian nymphs, tell your father the river
to quiet his current. Twine your hands in his beard,
and ask him to allow the children of Zeus
to be born in his water. Phthiótian Peneîos,
why are you racing the winds, old father? You are not   125
in a horse race. Are your feet always this fast,
or is it only for me you have become so athletic?"
He was deaf to her though.

                         "O my dear burden,
Where shall I bear you? My feet are worn out.   130
Pélion, wait! Remember Phílyra's marriage?
Please wait! Even wild lionesses
use your hills to give birth to raw cubs."

And awash with tears Peneîos replied:

"Leto, necessity is a great goddess.   135
I would never ignore your labor, Lady,
and I know of others who have washed
after birth in my waters. But Hera has
threatened me mercilessly. Look up
at the rock where a demon watches me.   140
He could easily pry me up from the depths.

What can I do? Would it give you pleasure
if Peneîos perishes? Well let the fated day come.
I'll bear it for you, even if I must
trickle away in droughty thirst eternal   145
and my fame be only most inglorious of rivers.
Here I am! What is left? Only call Eileithyîa."

He spoke, and checked his mighty current. But Ares
stood poised to wrench Mount Pangaîon up from its roots
heave it in the swirling waters and obliterate the river.   150
He let out a blood-curdling yell from the sky, smote
shield with spearpoint, and the vibrations shook Ossa,
the plain of Krannon quaked, ill winds scoured Pindos,
and all of Thessaly danced nervously. Thus the shield's
resonance and the aftershock's waves therefrom.   155
AS WHEN: Mount Aetna's cauldron smolders with fire
and shudders seismically when the moldering giant
Briáreos shifts restlessly to his other shoulder
and the forges of Hephaîstos rumble with the tumult
of tongs, tripods, and tempered basins falling and   160
banging against each other with the screech of steel,
SO NOW: the round shield rattled and boomed.
But Peneîos yielded not; he stood firm as before
and stopped his swift current, until Leto, daughter
of Koîos and Phoibê called to him: "Save yourself,   165
my friend, save yourself. You shouldn't suffer
for my sake. But I will repay your love and compassion."

Leto reached the islands with great labor,
but neither the Ekhínadês' calm harbor
nor hospitable Kerkýra would receive her;   170
Iris on high Mimas dissuaded them all
with her fierce anger; under her threat,
anyone Leto tried to reach in the currents
fled in fear. She came to primal Kos,
island of Merops, sanctuary of the heroine   175
Khalkíopê. But her child held her back
with this speech:

"Don't bear me here, mother.
    I don't blame
or complain against this island,   180
bright and rich in pasture as any other,
    but another god is due here from the Fates,
        of the Saviors' noble race;
two continents and the islands freely
will come to be ruled under a Macedonian crown,   185
        as far as the ends of earth
and wherever winged horses bear Helios;
and the son will follow his father's ways.

"Sometime later we will struggle side by side,
    when the latter-day Titans   190
        raise barbarian dagger,
Celtic Ares against the Hellenes
thick as snowflakes from the western verge,
numerous as stars portentous in the night,

[2 *lines missing*]

    the Krisaian plains overrun [195
       ] chasms of Hephaîstos [
resinous smoke, rumor of the enemy
hordes swarming over my temple,
    vile belts and shields of the mindless
Galatians deposited at Delphi,   200
other shields and their bearers in fire on the Nile,
trophies to mark the labor of a king,
                  O Ptolemy to come,
these prophecies of Phoîbos are yours,
these words from the womb yours to cherish   205
        all the days of your life.

"Mother be my sibyl:
    I see a slender island
wandering, her feet never still,
she swims through waves   210
    like flowering asphodel
blown by South Wind,

now by East,
wherever the sea bears her.
Carry me there. She will not reject you."   215

By the end of his speech, the islands were gone.
Astéria, song lover, you had come from Euboía
to the circular Cýcladês, not long ago,
still trailing the seaweed of Geraîstos.

[2 *lines missing*]

Seeing Leto weighed down with birth pains,   220
you called out:

"Hera, do what you want to me;
I disregard your threats.
Come, come to me Leto."

                    So you spoke.   225
Gratefully Leto stopped her sore wandering
and sat beside the stream of Ínopos,
which the earth sends out deepest when the full
Nile flows down from the Ethiopian cliffs.
She ungirded her robe, leaned her shoulders   230
against the trunk of a date palm, oppressed by
irrepressible pain, and sweat poured like rain
down her skin. Breathing hard, she cried:

"Why, child, do you weigh down your
mother? This is your island, dear,   235
floating on the sea. Be born, be born,
child, gently come out of my womb."

Bride of Zeus, heavy with anger, you soon heard
the news; a messenger ran to you, gasping
for breath, her words mixed with fear. She said: 240

"Honored Hera, most eminent of goddesses,
I am yours, everything is yours, you sit
lawful ruler of Olympos; we fear no other

female hand. And you, Queen, will know the author
of your anger: Leto ungirds her robe on an island.   245
All others shunned her, wouldn't welcome her,
but Astéria, drifting by, called out her name;
Astéria, evil refuse of the sea—you know her.
Dearest One, defend your slaves, Lady,
who walk the earth at your command."   250

And by the golden throne she sat like Artemis's
hound, who when the day's hunting is done,
crouches beside the Huntress's feet, her ears cocked,
always ready to welcome the Goddess's shout;
in the same way, the daughter of Thaumas crouches   255
by the throne. She never wanders from her place,
not even when sleep presses her with his wing
of forgetfulness, but leaning against the edge
of the great throne, her head slanting a little,
she sleeps. She never ungirds her robe   260
or swift boots, lest her mistress speak some
sudden word.

Hera's anger hung heavy in the air. She spoke:
"Now then, despicable creatures of Zeus,
you may marry secretly and give birth   265
in hidden places, where not even the miserable
slave who grinds grain suffers in childbirth
with difficult labor, but where ocean seals
bear on solitary sea-dashed rocks. I am not angry
with Astéria for erring, nor will I do   270
the unpleasant things I could, although
she gratified Leto quite wrongly; indeed, I
honor her because she did not trample on
my bed, but chose the sea instead of Zeus."

She spoke, and the swans, God's poets, sang;   275
they left Maiónian Paktólos circling Delos
seven times—the Muses' birds, most musical
of winged things—later the child strung
the lyre with seven strings, for the swans

sang over the birth pains that many times.   280
Before they could sing the eighth, Apollo
leapt out of the womb; the Delian nymphs,
daughters of ancient river, chanted the holy
song of Eileithyîa; the bronze air resounded
with the piercing cry. And Hera felt no   285
resentment because Zeus purged her anger.

Delos, then all your foundations became golden,
all day your round pool flowed with gold,
you native olive tree bore shoots of gold,
and deep, whirling Ínopos flooded with gold.   290
You lifted the child from the golden ground,
took him in your deep lap, and said something like this:

"O Great Mother Earth with all your altars and cities,
hear me, you rich continents and scattered
islands: I am hard to plow, but from me   295
Apollo will be called Delian; no other lands
will be so loved by other gods, not Kerkhnis by
Poseidon, lord of Lekhaeon, not Kyllénê's
hill by Hermes, not Crete by Zeus, as I
by Apollo; and I will wander no more."   300

You spoke, and Apollo sucked the sweet breast.
Ever since, you have been famous as the holiest island,
nursing-mother of Apollo; neither Énÿo nor Hades
nor the war-horses of Ares tread your land,
but each year tithes of first fruits are sent you;   305
each city brings choruses, those who have homes
toward Dawn, Hesperos, South, and the long-lived race
beyond the Northern sands.
                                      First, they bring you
cornstalks and holy sheaves of cornears, which come   310
from far-off lands to the Pelásgians of Dodóna
    (who sleep on the ground,
    servants of the never-silent gong);
next the offerings go to the holy town
and mountain of Mália;   315

from there they sail
to the good Lelantian Plain of the Abantes,
on Euboîa, a harbor neighboring your own.

Golden Arimáspians first brought you
these offerings: Oûpis and Loxo   320
and serene Hekaérgê, daughters of Boreas,
and the best young men of that time.
They never returned home, but were destined
for eternal fame: when the wedding song
echoes ominously in the women's quarters,   325
Delian girls offer a lock of hair
to their Arimáspian ancestors,
and Delian boys their first wisp of beard.

Astéria smoking with incense, round you the islands
have formed a circle, ranged like a chorus,   330
and not quiet or noiseless but ringed with sound,
curly haired Evening looks down on you ever,
the men sing the nome that the shaman Olen
brought centuries ago from Xanthos in Lykia,
and dancing women beat the earth with sure feet.   335
Then the sacred statue has its burden of garlands,
archaic Kypris's venerable image, established
by Theseus when he sailed back from Crete
with the youths he had saved from the Labyrinth
and the bellowing of Pasíphaë's monstrous son.   340

Round your altar, Lady, they raised the lute music
and danced the ring dance with Theseus leading.
And so the Athenians send the theoric offerings
aboard the Sacred Ship each year to Apollo.

Astéria with your many altars and rites, what merchant marine 345
sailing the Aegean would run his ship past you?
No matter how stiff the seabreeze is blowing
or how urgent his voyage, he furls his sail quickly
and does not board again until he has circled your altar
with his hands tied behind him, beaten with blows,   350

and has bitten the sacred olive's trunk. The Delian nymph
invented these games to amuse the boy-god Apollo.

Hail to you, happy hearth of the islands,
and hail to Apollo and to her whom Leto bore.

Hymn V: The Bath of Pallas

Prepare, ladies, the bath of Pallas.
Come,
I have heard the neighing of her holy horses,
Come,
The goddess will glide forth   5
Hurry,
my russet-haired Pelásgian ladies.
Athena never does bathe her long, shapely arms
before slapping the dust from her horses' flanks,
    not even when she bore her gear battle-grimed   10
    returning from war with the lawless Giants,
but first unbridled her chariot team
by the springs of Ocean and cleansed them from sweat,
    brightening their bits of all the jelled foam.

Ladies of Akhaîa, come!   15
but not with alabaster, not with myrrh
(I hear the whir of her axle now!)
no myrrh in alabaster for the bath of Pallas
    the goddess Athena does not wear perfume
and no mirror either: she is sure of her beauty.   20
Not even when Paris judged the contest on Ida
did the great goddess gaze into orichalch's glow
Or the diaphanous flow of the river Simóis.
Nor Hera,
    but Kypris gleamed with bronze reflections,   25
    cosmetic alterations of a woman and her hair,
while my goddess ran a two-hundred stade course
like the twin Spartan stars on the banks of Eurotas,
    then did her simple annointments:
    oil from her olive tree, applied with skill,   30
    and the blush, my dear maidens, that ran up her body
    was like dawn-rose and pomegranate.
Only this masculine, virgin oil
    (Herakles
    Kastor rubbed their bodies with olive)   35
and a golden comb for the Goddess's sleek hair.

Athena, come,
this company will please you,
these virgin children of Akéstor's great line,
Athena, come,   40
the ancient rite is begun,
Diomédes' shield is carried to Ínakhos,
an Argive rite taught by Eumédes,
                         your beloved priest
who fled crafty death with your holy icon   45
to the hill called Kreîon
                         and set you in rocks,
you, Pallas, on the Kreîon hill
                         in the rugged Pallatid rocks.

Athena, city destroyer,
Athena, helmeted in gold,   50
Athena, glad at the crash of horses and shields,

Come.

                         Today
the city will drink from small springs and fountains,
but not from the river;   55
girls will dip pitchers in Physadeîa today,
maidens bear water from Amýmonê's pool
                         (Danáos's daughter lives there)
For Ínakhos will flow from the shepherding hills
flooding his waters with flowers and gold,   60
this the fair bath of Pallas Athena.
                         But O
Pelásgian river,
                         brim your eyes to the queen:
the man who sees Pallas naked   65
                         holder of cities
                         sees Argos no more.
                         Come, Lady Athena, and
I will tell to your coming a myth not mine
for all these women: 70

There was a time in Thebes, my dears, Athena
    loved a nymph, loved her to distraction,
loved her more than any other, the mother
    of Tirésias, Kháriklo by name.
And they were always together: when Athena   75
    drove her horses to ancient Théspiai
or to Plataîa or Haliártos,
    riding through the farmlands of Boiótia,
or on to Koroneîa, where her grove is heavy
    with incense, and her altars lie close   80
to the river Kuríalos, it was goddess and nymph
    in one chariot together.
No party or dance was ever complete
    without Kháriklo there: then it was sweet.

But even for Kháriklo there were tears in store,   85
    dear as she was to Athena's heart.
One day these two unbuckled their robes.
    It was by Horse Spring, on Hélikon,
and the two were bathing in the beautiful creek.
    It was noon on the hill, dead calm, silent heat,   90
and they were bathing together. High noon. The hillside
    was steeped in awesome quiet,
and Tirésias was hunting, alone with his dogs,
    roaming that eerie hill.
                          He was young,   95
just bearded. Dry thirst led him down to the creek.
    And he stumbled upon the forbidden scene.
Controlling her anger, Athena spoke evenly:
    "Some god—which one, son of Evéres?—
has led you a rough road   100
    with an eyeless return."
And with her words night took the boy's eyes.
    He stood there, speechless, pain gluing his knees,
his voice paralyzed with shock. But the nymph screamed:

    "What have you done to my boy?   105
    Is this how goddesses
    show their friendship?

You've blinded him! O my poor baby,
you've seen the breast and thighs
    of Pallas Athena 110
but never the sunlight again.
Mountain of my sorrow, O Hélikon,
never will I set foot on you again.
You trade too hard,
    my son's eyes 115
for a few roe and deer!"

As she said this she cradled her son in her arms,
    mourning over him like a nightingale,
and led him away. But the goddess Athena
    pitied her friend and said this to her: 120

"You've spoken in anger, divine woman. Take back your words.
    It was not I who struck your son blind.
Putting out young eyes is not sweet to Athena,
    but the laws of Kronos demand
that whoever sees an immortal against the god's will 125
    must pay for the sight, and pay dearly.
What is done, divine woman, cannot be undone;
    this is the thread the Moirai spun
when you brought him to light. Now, son of Evéres,
    accept like a man what is only your due. 130
How many sacrifices would Autónoê burn,
    how many would Aristasîos, her husband,
to see their son Aktaion merely go blind?
    He will run in the company of great Artemis,
but neither their hunts in the hills together 135
    nor all of the arrows they'll shoot
will save him when he sees the bath of the goddess,
    not wanting to, mind you, but still his hounds
will chew their master to bits, and his mother will gather
    his bones from bushes all over the hill. 140
She will think you lucky and a fortunate woman
    to have your son home from the hills only blind.

"You musn't grieve so, darling. Your son will be honored,

all for your sake, by divine gift to him.
I'll make him a prophet, his fame will be mythic,   145
    the greatest prophet that ever has been:
He'll know all the birds in the sky, those of good omen
    and those whose flight presages doom.
He'll give oracles to the Boiótians, oracles to Kadmos,
    oracles to the mighty descendants of Lábdakos.   150
I will give him a great staff to guide his footsteps,
    and I will give him time, a long term of life,
and he alone, when he dies, will walk among the dead,
    wits intact, honored by Agesiláos, host of the dead."

When she had finished speaking Athena nodded her head,   155
    ensuring fulfillment of all that she said.
Pallas alone of all Zeus's daughters
    has received paternal prerogatives,
for no mother bore her, but the high brow of Zeus,
    and neither brow bends to affirm what is false,   160
[. . .]
O ladies who attend the bath of Pallas.

    And now the goddess comes,
                      Athena is coming.
Receive the goddess, receive her with prayers,
You who are chosen receive her rejoicing.   165
    Alleluia, Goddess, preserve Argos of Ínakhos,
    Alleluia, Goddess, when you drive out with horses,
    Alleluia, Goddess, when you drive them back home,
Save all the estate of the Danaans forever.

Hymn VI: To Demeter

Chant as the wicker moves in procession:
"Hail, great Earth Mother, lady of Grain!"
Chant, O my sisters, but if you are not an initiate,
Watch from the ground, not from rooftop or height,
Child, woman, or flowing-haired girl—not then nor when   5
We spit from dry mouths in the ritual fast.
Hesperos watches from the clouds for its coming,
Hesperos who alone convinced Deo to drink
When she searched for the footprints of her ravaged daughter.
How could your feet carry you, Lady, to the West,   10
The black men, the gloomgolden apples? You did not
Drink, eat, or bathe the whole time you traveled.
Three times you crossed the silverslipping streams
Of Akhéloös and each of the perpetual rivers.
Three times by Kallíkhoros Spring you sat down,   15
Parched on the ground without drinking water,
Nor did you eat or bathe in the pool.

But we will not speak of what brought tears to Deméter.
Prettier to tell how she gave cities fair laws,
How she was the first to cut straw, bind   20
Holy sheaves, and put the oxen to tread them
When she taught Triptólemos the good art of farming.
A prettier poem, and a grim warning to all,
To tell how she wasted the son of Triópas.

The Pelásgians still lived in Old Thessaly then   25
And had made for the goddess a beautiful grove
With trees so close scarcely an arrow could pass,
Pine and great elms, sweet apples and pears,
And water foamed up in the trenches like amber.
She was mad for the place, loved it like Eleusis   30
Or Triopa, or Enna. But fortune turned sour
For the clan of Triópas, and Erysíkhthon lost
His sense of good judgment. He armed twenty retainers
With axes and hatchets, great hulks of men
who could lift a whole town, and stampeded them into   35

Deméter's holy grove. A poplar grew there,
A tree that kissed the blue sky: woodnymphs played
In its shadow at noon. It was the first to be hit
And keened to the others a cadenza of pain.
Deméter knew her holy wood was in danger. She cried out   40
In anger, "Who is felling my beautiful trees?"
And appeared on the scene disguised as Nikíppê,
Her public priestess by the city's appointment,
A poppy clenched in her hand, the key of office
Slung over her shoulder, and dealt with him gently,   45
Trying to reason with the sacrilegious oaf:

"My child, why are you cutting the trees of the gods?
Stop this, my son. Your parents hoped better for you.
Cease, and order your men to desist, before Lady Deméter
Becomes angry with you for destroying her shrine."   50

He looked at her with a scowl more ferocious
Than a birth-raw lioness gives to a hunter
In the Tmárian hills: No glare is more baleful.
"Out of my way, or I'll bury this axe in your chest!
This timber will roof me a fine drinking hall   55
Where my friends and I will feast forever."
An ugly speech from the lad, and Nemesis duly

Recorded his words. Now Deméter's anger
Transcended speech: she was the Goddess once more,
Her feet firm on terra, her head level with Olympos.   60
The men were half-dead with fear when they saw the grim
Lady, and ran away leaving bronze axes in oaks.
She let them go, a despot's mere underlings
And addressed instead their ponderous lord:
"O yes, yes, you dog, go build a hall   65
For feasting with friends. Your feasts will come fast now."

And with these words she wrought Erysíkhthon's doom,
Infecting him with a virulent hunger, a caloric
Morbidity, an astringent disease that puckered his innards,
An appetite unabated no matter how much he ate.   70

Twenty servants prepared his dinner, and twelve
Poured the wine (Dionýsos always supports Deo's grudges:
What affronts Deméter affronts the Wine God as well).
His mortified parents invented every excuse
Not to send him to dinner parties. The sons of Órmenos   75
Summoned him to Athena's Itónian Games.
His mother demurred: "He's not home. He just went
to Krannon to collect a debt of twenty oxen."
Polýxo came, Aktórian's mother, with a wedding invitation
For Triópas and son. Fighting back tears, the lady replied: 80
"Triópas will come. Erysíkhthon a boar wounded
Up on Mount Pindos. He's been nine days in bed."
The poor woman loved her son. Why shouldn't she lie?
Another neighbor was giving a feast: "I'm sorry,
But Erysíkhthon left the country today." Another marriage: 85
"A discus hit Erysíkhthon," or "He fell off his horse,"
Or "He's out on Mount Othrys counting his sheep."

While inside the house the incessant gourmand
Ate round the clock, and the more he ate,
The more his stomach somersaulted for more.   90
It was as if the victuals were poured in the sea
And the abyss didn't burble a bubble of thanks.
Like snow on Mount Mimas, like a wax doll in the sun,
He melted to sinews. Nerve-strings and bones
Were all that remained. His mother cried, his sisters   95
Both groaned, as did his old nurse and ten faithful servants.
Old man Triópas pulled his white hair and addressed
To Poseîdon, his putative father by Kanáke, the nymph,
Words that Poseîdon affected not to hear:

"Some patriarch you are! Look at your grandson!   100
Better Apollo should shoot him and I lay him to rest.
My son the ox-eater. So cure him—you're a god—
Or take him and feed him yourself! My pantry's exhausted,
My stables are empty, my cooks have all quit!
He's eaten the wagon mules, the cow that his mother   105
Was fattening for Hestia, the thoroughbred, the war-horse,
Even the cat—and such a mouser he was!"

So long as Triópas's estate had supplies,
Only the walls were aware of the scandal.
But when his teeth had weeviled to the house's depths,   110
The king's son was reduced to sitting at crossroads
Begging for crusts, leftovers, and garbage.

May I never be friends with your enemies, Goddess,
May no wall unite us. I loathe bad neighbors.

Sing, maidens, and join the chant, mothers: 115
    "Hail, great Earth Mother, Lady of Grain!"
And as four white horses carry the basket,
May the wide-ruling goddess whiten our harvest
And so preserve us through white winter and spring
And the white heat of summer. As we walk the city   120
Without sandals or snoods, so may our heads
Be safe from all harm and our feet protected.
As we carry baskets filled with gold grain,
So may we be showered with gold.

                    The uninitiated   125
May follow as far as the Prytaneîon,
The initiates to the goddess's shrine,
But those who are heavy with age or with child
Or the women in pain may come just as far
As their knees will allow: Deméter will give them   130
As full a share as if they had come to the temple.

Hail, Goddess, and save this city,
Keep it harmonious and prosperous ever,
Bring good things home to us from the fields,
Feed our cattle, bring us more flocks,   135
Bring us ears of grain, bring in the harvest!
And nourish peace, Goddess, so that he who plows
May also reap.
          And be gracious to me, Goddess,
Thrice prayed for, Great Queen.   140

EPIGRAMS

I

News of your death.

Tears, and the memory
of all the times we talked the sun down the sky.

You, Herakleîtos of Halikarnássos,
once my friend, now vacant dust,
    whose poems are nightingales
beyond the clutch of the unseen god.

2

"Timónoë."
            Who are you, lady,
    besides a name on a tombstone
determined by other names:
                            Timótheos,
your father, and Methýmna,
    your city, and your husband,
Euthýmenes,
            widowed and grieving.

3

The demon in the morning,
Unknown. Yesterday, Kharmis,
You were in our eyes. Today
We buried you. Yes, Kharmis,
You. Nothing
Your father has ever seen
Has caused him more pain.

4

Shipwrecked stranger, Leóntikhos found your
Anonymous corpse and gave you burial
On the seabeach here. His tears, though, were for
His own mortality. Restless sailor,
He beats over the sea like a flashing gull.

5

Dawn came like a black horse
And we buried young Melaníppos.

At nightfall his sister Básilo died:
Unendurable, her brother on the pyre.

The family stared at two deaths
And the town bowed her head

For the desolate house
And the children dead.

6

The young girls of Samos
Are looking for Krêthis,
Their sweetest playmate,
With her chatter and games.
But Krêthis must sleep now,
The sleep that finally
Quiets every young girl.

7

Stranger, know that I who rest here
Was once a priestess of Deméter,

And priestess too of the Kabíri,
And later also of Kybélê;

That this old woman, now dust in earth,
Helped many through the pains of birth

And bore two sons, in whose arms I
Closed my eyes. Farewell. Pass by.

8

If sailing vessels had never been,
We would not be mourning Diokleîdes' son.
But Sópolis's corpse is adrift on the sea,
And we pass by a name on an empty tomb.

9

Mikkos kept his Phrygian nurse Aîskhra
Well cared for all her life, and when she died
Set up her statue in perpetual gratitude
For the old woman and her nursing breasts.

10

Spare means, modest life,
Injustice to none.

If I, Míkylos, ever condoned
Any wrongdoing, press hard on my bones,

Earth and you spirits
Who rest on my tomb.

II

If you seek Timarkhos in Hades' house
    To learn of the soul and how *you* shall fare,
Inquire for the son of Pausanias
    Among the righteous—you will find him there.

12

Sáon of Akánthos
Son of Díkon
In awesome, perfect sleep here lies.
Deny forever that the good man dies.

13

If you go to Kýzikos it will be easy to find
    Dídymê and Hippákos: their house is not obscure.
And it will be hard news to tell, yet tell them this:
    I cover their son here, their Krítias.

14

Tread by the tombstone
Of Kimon of Elis
And know that you pass
the child of Hippaîos.

15

He was twelve years old when his father laid him here,
    Philip's great hope, his son Nikóteles.

16

This is the grave of the father and son
Of Callímachus. You will know the one
As general of Kyréné's armed might.
The other's poems prevailed against Spite.

17

Here lies Battos's son. His line
Was verse, his diversion wine.

18

Menékrates of Aînos, noble guest
Too briefly with us, what laid you to rest?
Was the Centaur's doom your undoing too?

"Wine was my curse, but death came when due."

19

Here lies Timon, misanthrope *par excellence*.
Curse me as you pass, but pass by at once.

20

Pass by, hypocrite, and no "fond farewell" stuff.
For you not to mock me is farewell enough.

21

Which do you hate more, Timon, darkness or light?

"Darkness: there are more of you down here to spite."

22

He stooped to put flowers on his stepmother's tomb,
Thinking she'd changed since meeting her doom.

He died when her gravestone fell on his head.
Stepmothers are dangerous even when dead.

23

The gentleman was curt
And his epitaph brief:

THERIS • SON OF ARISTAÎOS • OF CRETE

But it is still too much
For his tombstone to bear.

24

"Is Kháridas beneath this stone?"
"Yes, if you mean Arrímas's son
From Kyrénê, I'm his tomb."

"Kháridas, what's it like below?"
"Dark." "Are there exits?" "None."
"And Pluto?" "He's a myth." "Oh, no!"

"All that I'm telling you is true,

But if you want the bright side too,
The cost of living here is low."

25

Astákides, the Cretan goatherd,
Was swept off the hill
By a nymph in heat
And is now a cult hero.

Daphnis no longer
Under Diktê's oaks
Shall we shepherds sing.
Only Ass-
        taaakides now.

26

Kleómbrotos of Ambrákia said "Farewell,
Sun," and leaped from a high wall clear into Hell.
He had no serious problems, as far as we know,
But had just finished reading Plato's *Phaedo*.

27

Lykos of Naxos died
No onshore death, but spied
Both ship and soul going down
At sea. He was bound
Out of Aigína in a freighter
And is now a corpse in the water,
While I, his grave with a name
And nothing else proclaim
The all too-true maxim:
                        Remember,
Sailor, not to get wet

When the Goat Stars set
   At dawn in December.

28

I am an old shell,
            O Lady of Zephýrion,
But now I am yours, Kypris,
   Selenaîa's first offering.

Once I was a nautilus, sailing
The seas when the winds blew,
My body both seaman and ship.
But when Calm, that sleek goddess,
Came, I rowed hard with my feet
(You see how well named I was)
Until I beached on the sand dunes
Of Iulis, so to become, my Arsínoë,
Your curious toy, and no more
To bear in my chambers the moist
Kingfisher's eggs.
            Nautilus is becalmed.

But do thou, Goddess, give grace
   To the daughter of Kleînias.
She is intelligent and does everything well,
   And she comes from Aiólian Smyrna.

29

Four Graces now, for to the Three
One has been added, just modeled
And still wet with perfume:
            Blest, radiant Bereníkê,
Without whom the very Graces are graceless.

In the temple of Isis, daughter of Ínakhos,
Stands an ikon of Aískylis, daughter of Thales,
In fulfillment of the vow to her mother, Eirénê.

Philerátis dedicated
This image to Artemis.
Accept it,
                    Lady,
And watch over her safety.

Come once again, Eileithyîa,
When Lykaínis calls you,
And deliver her lightly
From the pains of childbirth,
So as now for a girl, later too
For a boy, Goddess, your fragrant
Temple may possess a new gift.

Kallístion,
            daughter of Krítias,
dedicated me,
            a twenty-nozzle lamp,
to the God of Kanópos,
            ornate votive offering
for her child Apéllis.
                        See me lit
and exclaim,
            "The Evening Star has fallen!"

34

Ménitas, the Lýktian,
Dedicated his archery gear
Saying: "The hornbow
And quiver I present to you,
Sarapis. The arrows
The men of Hésperis have."

35

I am a dedicatory hero,
Set near the doors of Eëtion,
Of Trojan descent, small
Statue in a small vestibule,
Sword and snake, no more,
In particular no mount,
Eëtion still being touchy
About artificial horses.

36

To Deméter of the Gates,
For whom the Pelásgian
Akrísios built this shrine,
And to her Daughter below,

Timodémos of Naúkratis
Here offers and dedicates
Ten percent of his profits,
According to contract.

37

To the Gods of Samothrace
Eudémos here dedicates

The saltcellar, whose spare
Seasoning saved him from
Squalls of billowing bills:

Ex votis, safe now from salt.

38

Mikkos's boy Simos dedicated me,
A mask of Dionýsos, beseeching
The Muses that his lessons come easy,
And the goddesses, like Glaukos,
Gave him golden ease of learning
For his brass. Meanwhile, I,
A tragic Dionýsos, sit here outyawning
The Gaping God of Samos, and listen
To brats recite from the BACCHAE,
"Sacred is the hair, etc.," repeating
Ad nauseam my own dream to me.

39

Call me Pámphilos,
      comic witness
to the victory of Agoránax,
      the Rhodian playwright,
grossly comic: not just
      the usual love-wracked mask,
but one side crinkled like
roasted figs
      and the nozzled lamps of Isis.

40

Be advised, Asklépios:
You have collected the debt

Contracted by Akéson
For his wife, Demódikê.
If you forget and demand
Payment again, this tablet
Agrees to be Exhibit A.

41

Goats of Mount Kynthos:
    Cretan Ekhémmas
Has dedicated to Artemis
The bow that he used
To clear the mountain of you.
    He and the Goddess
Have agreed to a truce.

42

O Lion-strangling, Boar-slaying Lord, to thee
I am offered, the branch of an oak tree,
By—"Whom?"—Arkhínos—"Which one?"—from Crete—
"Oak branch accepted, dedication complete."

43

Euainétos erected me
and says
    (how could I know,
being a bronze cock?)
        that in return
for some personal
conquest, I am dedicated
to Kastor and Polydeûkes.

I believe the son of Phaîdros,
        son of Philoxénides.

44

Simónê the streetwalker dedicated
To Aphrodite the following gifts:

A portrait of herself,
The brassiere that kissed her breasts,
And, well, other accoutrements
Of her wretched profession.

45

The hunter in the hills
    tracks down
every hare and every roe
    crackling on
through frost and snow.
If someone says
"Here's a beast already shot,"
He leaves it there.
So too my lust
    pants to chase
what runs away
    but flits on past
what's there to stay.

46

By Pan and Dionýsos, there's still
Fire beneath these ashes! But my
Heart's not in it. Don't get me involved.
Nobody notices the quiet river
Undermining the wall; and I'm afraid,
Menéxenos, that this dog-eyed boy might
Slip in and knock me for a loop into Love.

47

Pour another round and toast Diokles!
No Akhéloös River water in these
Sacred cups. 's a lovely boy though, Akhéloös,
No? Then leave his loveliness all to me.

48

If that dusky beauty
                    Theókritos
Rejects me, Lord Zeus, despise him four-square;
But love him if he loves me,
                    In the name
Of Ganymédê, whose long, fine hair
Once excited your lust.
                    Here I end my prayer.

49

If I sang at your door willingly,
Arkhínos, go ahead and blame me,
But if I sang under duress,
Don't accuse me of rashness.
Straight wine and the love-god
Forced me: one pulled, the other allowed
No self-restraint. And when I came
I didn't bawl out, "'s anybody in?"
No, I pressed my lips to the doorframe.
If that's a sin, well then, I've sinned.

50

I know my hands are empty
Of gifts, but by the Graces
Don't tell me my own dream.

It's torture to hear such
Taunts from you, Menippos,
And so unloverlike of you, my dear.

51

Kleoníkos of Thessaly, by the Sun
I hardly recognized you. Why you're
Nothing but skin and bones! What
Have you been up to, you poor twit?
Did you make the same mistake I did?
Aha!
Caught by Euxítheos! You paid a visit
To that gorgeous creature and had the nerve
To look at him with both eyes wide open.

52

on the 20th of june i said,
"it's all over, Menékrates, get out
while you can," and what do you know,
on the—what was it—10th of july
the ox came to the plow all by itself,
and i said, "that's my boy, Hermes,
that's my boy, and never you mind
about the twenty-day late charge."

53

Half my soul's still breathing well,
Half's in love or gone to hell,
I can't tell which, but probably
It's trafficking in pederasty,
Although I told those boys, "Steer clear,
Don't let that runaway come near!"

I know it's flirting there, the flit,
Somebody help me hunt for it!

54

Kallignótos to Iónis swore
He'd never love a woman more,
Nor any man, than he loved her.
They say such oaths don't register
In immortal ears. So with this vow:
Kallignótos lusts after boys now,
And the girl—a Delphic twist—
She isn't even on his list.

55

That mysterious stranger
Tried to conceal his wound,
But what a heart-wrenching sigh
When he finished his third round,

And did you see how the carnation
Fell out of his lapel?
He's a thief who's been burned.
I'm a thief, I can tell.

56

Polyphémos (O that Cyclops was smart) discovered
    a beautiful charm for the lovelorn:
The Muses, dear Philip, can bring down Love's swelling,
    and the poet's art is pure panacea.
Then consider the compensatory virtue in hunger:
    it cures attacks of boy-love just like that.
So we have two forms of therapy for your neurosis, Eros,
    and you can just get your wings clipped, little boy.

We don't care a crumb for you now that we have
　　both these home remedies to treat your trauma.

57

Konópion, I hope you sleep
the way you make me, your lover,
lie on this freezing porch.
I hope you sleep
　　　　　　　—you're so unfair!—
as you make your lover lie. You
wouldn't know pity if you met it
in a dream. Even the neighbors
pity me. You, not even in a dream.
But your hair turned gray, Konópion,
will bring all this back to you some day.

58

I hate the poems in the Epic Cycle, I don't like highways
　　that are heavily traveled, I despise
a promiscuous lover, and I don't drink from public fountains:
　　Everything public disgusts me. And yes, Lysánias,
you are handsome as handsome, but before I can even say it,
　　back comes the echo: "Some other man has him."

59

Theaitétos traveled
An immaculate path
Even if it led not
To Bakkhos's dark ivy.

Heralds will intone
Other names brief moments,

All Hellas resound
His poetry forever.

60

Very few words from the prize-winning playwright:
"I won." Short and sweet.
But, Dionýsos, if you breathe
Bad luck, the loser will say:
"It's hard to believe things turned out this way . . ."
Pentameter speech of a desperate man.
Make mine monometer, Lord, if you can.

61

The sad mad hero of old Orestes,
Dear Leúkaros, at least had the sense
Not to put his Phókian friend
To the ultimate test: producing one play
Would surely have meant their friendship's end.
It's how I've lost all my old Pýladae.

62

Arátos of Soloi models his verse
On Hesiod's best, and refuses to write
The Ultimate Epic. We praise these terse,
Subtle tokens of long effort at night.

63

Homer's Samian host Kreóphylos authored me,
     Epic of Iólê and Eúrytos's woe.
Some edit me with Homer's poetry:
     Zeus, this is great news for Kreóphylos though!

64

Píttakos of Mytilénê, Hyrrhas's son,
Was questioned once by an Atárneian:
"Two brides are proposed to me, reverend sir,
And I need your advice on which to prefer.
One is my equal in birth and estate,
The other's above me. Which should I mate?"
Lifting the staff that propped his old age,
"Those children will tell you," answered the sage.
Out in the crossroads some boys were at play
Racing their tops. "Heed what they say!"
The Atárneian drew near and heard the boys' refrain
As they lashed their tops: "Stay in your own lane!"
It was all he needed to make him decide
He'd better forgo the lucrative bride.
And just as that man took a bride at no gain,
So should you, Dion,
Stay in your own lane.

FRAGMENTS

Prologue to the Aetia

The malignant gnomes who write reviews in Rhodes
    are muttering about my poetry again—
tone-deaf ignoramuses out of touch with the Muse—
because I have not consummated a continuous epic
    of thousands of lines on heroes and lords   5
but turn out minor texts as if I were a child
    although my decades of years are substantial.
To which brood of cirrhotic adepts
               I, Callímachus, thus:

A few distichs in the pan outweigh *Deméter's Cornucopia,*   10
    and Mimnermos is sweet for a few subtle lines,
not that fat *Lady* poem. Let "cranes fly south to Egypt"
    when they lust for pygmy blood,
and "the Masságetai arch arrows long distance"
    to lodge in a Mede,   15
but nightingales are honey-pale
    and small poems are sweet.
So evaporate, Green-Eyed Monsters,
or learn to judge poems by the critic's art
    instead of by the parasang,   20
and don't snoop around here for a poem that rumbles:
    not I but Zeus owns the thunder.

When I first put a tablet on my knees, the Wolf-God
    Apollo appeared and said:
"Fatten your animal for sacrifice, poet,   25
    but keep your muse slender."
And
    "follow trails unrutted by wagons,
don't drive your chariot down public highways,
    but keep to the back roads though the going is narrow.   30
We are the poets for those who love
    the cricket's high chirping, not the noise of the jackass."

A long-eared bray for others, for me delicate wings,
    dewsip in old age and bright air for food,

mortality dropping from me like Sicily shifting   35
   its triangular mass from Enkélados's chest.
No nemesis here:
        the Muses do not desert the gray heads
   of those on whose childhood
            their glance once brightened.   40

Aetia

[...]

   when the Muses settled like a swarm of bees
near Hesiod, out on the hill with his sheep,
    by the fiery horse's hoofprint
         generation out of Chaos
     water from the hoof

"hurt another and hurt yourself most"

    to live worthily
       all things you accomplish

             accomplish

[...]

Victory of Bereníkê

FRAGMENT I

[...]
I owe a gift of thanksgiving to Zeus and Neméa,
    Bereníkê, Bride, holy sister of gods:
my victory song [   ] your mares.
    Fresh from the land of Danaans born of Io
to Helen's isle and the Pallenê seer, Proteus,   5
    shepherd of seals, came golden news:

that beside the hill of Ophéltes
    your horses ran in front; no other charioteers,
panting, warmed their shoulders, and divine
    like the wind they saw no trace of wheels.   10
[
    and before at Argos [young women wove]
finely spun tapestries [more skillfully than]
    Kolkhian or Egyptian women [who with great
art] worked delicate weavings [so]
    women knowing to bewail the white-flecked bull   15
          ] when [it commemorates your victory
will marvel at your tapestry]
[...]

FRAGMENT 2

[...]
to strife when [
    a man of Tanágra gave [
for his brother's child [20
    how constrained [
Taphian's property [
    fleece [
flying [
    overthrown [25
while bound [
    [
the bow split [
    And Herakles said to Molórkhos: [

"Thistles and brambles [   ] by me [
    [
wild pear by the house [30
    I pulled out from the stone pile [
if you told me about all this [   ]."
    He spoke and Molórkhos replied:
"May your former prayer [
    be granted, the robber [35
terrible lion might destroy [
    and god grant you either kill [
so I can get wood for a fire and feed you
              ] and not lack fuel.
        ] Now unpruned young trees [40
        ] bounding [   ] passes this month [
        ] Longing to bite the medicago the nanny goat
        ] bleats, shut within the gates [
        ] nor does the smelly billy's kid
        ] shudder to see the eagle [45
        ] but with flocks eager for pasture [
        ] sitting idle as if beseiged [
        ] not, as they say, to [deceive Kronos]
        ] Rheîa gave birth to a stone [
[
        ] Hera, no longer patroness [50
        ] of Argos [
[. . .]

FRAGMENT 3

[. . .]
            ] raising a forked branch
            ] house, not even [
            ] alloting a portion for his child.
When the evening star, who comes at sunset,
    began to release yokes from the oxen,
        ] when the sun shines on Óphion's progeny,
        ] the older gods
        ] the door, but he heard a noise
    like the roar of a lion cub to a timid deer,   60
at least that loud,

he heard it and whispered:
"Thieves, why do you come again,
    neighbors wearing out our house,
since you certainly bring nothing?   65
    God made you a curse to hosts."
Saying this he threw down his work [
    he crafted a tricky device for mice
and in two traps placed deadly bait
        ] taking meal of darnel mixed with hellebore   70
            ] he hid death
[

            ] as hawks [   ] swooping
    often they gathered oil from the lamp,
drawing it out with their tails in leaps
    when the lid was not in place,   75
or they stole from another coffer
    even a poor man's goods,
    ] from under a stone fell on the bed
    ] dancing on his head, driving sleep from his eyes.
But what enraged him most, the ravening beasts   80
    shamelessly committed in one short night:
the monsters gnawed through his clothes,
    a goat's hair cloak and pouch;
for them he devised double death:
    a long mousetrap, cunning to catch   85
        ] he opened the door
[

        ] after that he often mixed
[. . .]

FRAGMENT 4

[. . .]
            ] Zeus, because of your poverty [
            ] they are guiltless [
            ] never have I given a lyre [90
            to me, old man [
[. . .]

FRAGMENT 5

[...]
    ] paragon of monsters [
or I must call him the bane of Argives
    ] by roaring [
    ] beside the great well of Danáos   95
    ] Melampos obtained for his brother [
    ] washing [   ] to cure impotence [
    ] if only I could get my club near [
    ] you would soon own oxen,
    ] even though the odds are against me [100
    ] I shall prove that Zeus fathered a son,
    ] but if I fall beneath its teeth,
    ] sacrifice [
[
    ] your ox to me [
    ] given by gods [105
[. . .]

FRAGMENT 6

[...]
You may imagine it yourself
        and cut away my song's length,
  but I will tell all that Herakles replied:
"Old father, the rest you will learn at the feast,
  but now you will hear what Pallas told me [110
[...]

FRAGMENT 7

[...]
and they will not win a race horse or ox-sized
  cauldron [
    ] but a parsley crown [
    ] when [
    ] of gold [115
  and the Corinthians, holding games
much older than those near Poseîdon's sanctuary,
  will set a token of the Isthmian victory

in rivalry with Neméan and slight the pine
    that owned the competitors in Ephýra.   120
       ] your mule, old man [
       ] nor holy [

[
       ] Pallas [

[
       ] named after her [
       ] and Molórkhos [125
       ] pleasing his guest's appetite [
He stayed overnight and left early for Argos.
    Nor did he forget the promise to his host:
he sent the mule and honored him as kin.
    Now the ritual never will cease   130
       ] Pelops [
       ] held [
       ] set up [
       ] child [
[. . .]

FRAGMENT 8

[. . .]
    The furious wife of Zeus spewed up the lion   135
to destroy Argos, though it was her city,
    to be a harsh labor for Zeus's bastard.
[. . .]

FRAGMENT 9

[. . .]
    The lion skin his veil,
a defense against snow and arrows [
[. . .]

FRAGMENT 10

[. . .]
Hanging from his shoulder the lion skin   140
[. . .]

Akóntios and Kydíppê

Eros taught Akóntios, when the boy
burned for lovely Kydíppê, the skill

(he wasn't crafty) to win the virgin
to be his wedded wife. He came from Iúlis

(Euxántios's blood) and she from Naxos   5
(kin to Promethes) to your ox sacrifice,

Kynthian Lord, in Delos: two radiant
stars of the islands. Mothers offered

many oxen for Kydíppê, still a child,
betrothal gifts on behalf of their sons.   10

No other girl with a face more like
morning appeared at shaggy Silénos's

dewy springs, or set a lighter foot
in the dance of sleeping Ariádnê.

FRAGMENT 68

lovers watched when the youth   15
left for school or the bath

FRAGMENT 69

and many wine-drinking lovers of Akóntios
tossed their wine dregs to the ground
in the Sicilian game

FRAGMENT 70

but the archer himself   20
felt an arrow from another's bow

FRAGMENT 72

he wandered to the country on every pretext

FRAGMENT 73

but may your bark bear so many engraved letters
that say: BEAUTIFUL KYDÍPPÊ

FRAGMENT 75

Already Kydíppê bedded down with the boy: 25
the ritual prenuptial sleep for the bride

with a young boy whose parents were alive.
For they say once Hera—hold it right there

you dog of a poet! you would sing
sacrilege; good thing you haven't seen   30

dread Deméter's rites or you would've belched out
even their story. Excessive knowledge

is an unwieldy ill; a man with a loose
tongue is indeed a child with a knife.

Next morning, the oxen would have torn their hearts,   35
seeing the blade reflected in the water,

but in the evening, damp evil seized her
(disease falsely called holy, exorcized

onto wild goats)—and the epilepsy
wasted Kydíppê nearly to Hades.   40

A second time the beds were made; again
she labored seven months with quartan fever.

A third time they remembered marriage;
again cold death settled on Kydíppê.

A fourth—her father waited no longer,   45
but asked Phoîbos, who answered in the night:

"Your child's oath to Artemis is frustrating
her marriage; for my sister wasn't troubling

Lygdámis or weaving reeds in Amyklaía
or rinsing stains in the Parthénios River   50

after hunting, but was at home in Delos
when your child swore to marry no other

but Akóntios. Kéÿx, as your counselor
I say fulfill your daughter's oath—

You won't mix lead with silver, but electrum   55
with brilliant gold. You, the father-in-law,

are descended from Kodros; the Kean
bridegroom from priests of Zeus Aristaîos

in Íkmios, whose mountain ministry
appeases baleful Sirius rising,   60

and begs Zeus for winds that hurl flocks
of quail into the cloudlike linen nets."

The god spoke, and Kéÿx returned to Naxos.
He questioned his daughter, who revealed

the truth and again was well. Akóntios,   65
you came to Naxos; Kydíppê's companions

sang her wedding song without delay; the oath
to the goddess was kept. I don't think you,

Akóntios, would trade Íphikles' feet
skimming over cornears or Kelainaîan   70

Midas's wealth, for the night you touched her
virgin belt; anyone would agree who knows

stern Eros. From this marriage a great name
arose: your tribe, the Akontiádai,

live abundant and honored at Iúlis.   75
I heard of your love from old Xenomédes,

who once compiled a mythological
record of the whole island, beginning

with Korýkian nymphs from Parnassos,
pursued by a lion to the island,   80

thus called Hydrússa; the Karians and
Léleges settled it, whose offerings

Zeus Alaláxios always receives with
the trumpet's war cry, and Keos, son of

Phoîbos and Mélia, changed it to his name.   85
The old man put it all in his tablets: violence,

thunderbolt death, wizard Telkhínes,
Demónax ignoring the blessed gods,

aged Mákelo, Dexíthea's mother,
(who alone the immortals left unscathed   90

when they sank the island for its sins),
and Keos's four cities: Mégakles built Karthaîa;

Eúpylos, half-divine Khryso's son,
the city of many fountains, Iúlis;

Akaios, seat of the Graces, Poiéssa;   95
and Aphrástos build little Korésos.

Melded with this, the truthful old man recorded
the tale of your poignant love, Kean; from there

the story of Kydíppê ran to Kallíopê,
    Muse of Callímachus.   100

The Lock of Bereníkê

Konon the astronomer, who has observed every star
    in the sky, determined their risings and settings,
is the expert on solar eclipses, the corona's splendor,
    the slow precession of the constellations,
and into what cave on Latmos the Moon-Goddess descends   5
    when love's librations disturb her orbit—
this Konon has also observed in the velvet night sky
    yours truly, a lock of hair from Bereníkê's head,
glowing serenely, which she dedicated to All Goddesses,
    stretching out her slender arms in supplication,   10
what time the king, her newlywed husband, sated and proud,
    sallied forth to annex Syria to his realm,
displaying, I might add, on his royal person the marks
    of the previous night's struggle for virgin spoils.
Query: Is Aphrodite really distasteful to brides? Are those   15
    crocodile tears they shed at the bridal chamber's threshold,
blubbering away while their parents are weeping for joy?
    Dissimulated groans, so help me gods,
as I deduced from my mistress's pitiful lamentations
    the day her new husband went off to war.   20
Oh, but you say you weren't mourning your desolate bed
    but the poignant departure of a cherished brother?
And yet the sorrow consumed you down to the marrow,
    your bosom heaved with exquisite anxiety,
you were senseless with grief! And this from a woman   25
    I've known as courageous from girlhood on.
Or have you forgotten the noble crime by which you secured
    your royal marriage? Who else would have dared it?
What a fit of *tristesse*, what a maudlin send-off you gave him!
    Zeus! how many times did your hanky dab your eyes?   30
A character change wrought by some god? Or do lovers
    simply resent the absence of the body loved?
Anyway, you dedicated me to All Goddesses (with a good deal
    of bull's blood) toward your husband's return,
and return he did, in fairly short order, having annexed   35
    half of Asia to his eastern frontier.

For which exploits and in expiation of which vow
    I have been enrolled a member of this celestial club.

Under protest, my Queen, have I withdrawn from Your Eminence!
    Under protest, I swear by you and your head   40
(And may he get his just deserts who takes your crown in vain).
    But who can claim to be equal to Iron?
Even monstrous Mount Athos, the greatest promontory
    under the sun (bright son of Thia)
was likewise uprooted when the Persians canalled it   45
    and the barbarian fleet sailed through a new sea.
What valence has hair besides such elements as Iron?
    May the tribes of the Khálybes perish from earth
along with the inventor of shaft mining, their blacksmith friends
    and the first stinking smelter with his load of pig iron.   50
My sister strands, just recently parted, were bewailing my fate,
    When Memnon's brother, Arsínoë's dainty mount, pumping
dappled wings, whisked me away through the ethereal dark
    and deposited me in Aphrodite's chaste lap.
Zephyrítis herself had commissioned this flight,   55
    the Hellenic lady who haunts Egypt's shores.
And Aphrodite, lest the crown form Ariádnê's temples
    be the only such fixture to light the night sky,
arranged that I too, blonde consecrated spoils dripping
    with tears, should illumine the precincts divine,   60
installing me as a new constellation 'midst the old.
    Bordering on Virgo's and ferocious Leo's
stars, and extending to Kallísto, the Arkadian Bear,
    I wheel to the West, preceding slow Boötes.
Boötes who but slowly sinks into deep Ocean.   65
    Yet though all night I reel under the feet of the gods,
Dawn ever returns me to the mystic, white sea.

    And now, Virgin Nemesis, forgive me
for the outspoken candor of what I feel I must say,
    And may the stars spare me their scalding gossip: 70
I am not so happy with this state of affairs that I don't
    suffer terribly at the permanent separation
from my mistress's head, together with whom I have imbibed

perfumes galore (though we abstained when she was a virgin).
So this is my plea: 75
                    You virgins blessed by the bridal torch,
     before offering your bodies to your ardent husbands,
before you even pull off your dress to bare your nipples,
     offer me some ointment from your onyx jar—
but only if you're devoted to what a chaste bed allows.   80
     If any adulteress should pour a libation,
may dry dust soak it up and render it void. I want
     no propitiation from disreputable women.
My wish is rather that conjugal harmony inhabit
     the homes of all brides, and constant devotion.   85
And you, my Queen,
                    when on your way with festal lamps
     to appease Aphrodite you look up at the stars,
do not allow me, once yours, to remain unperfumed,
     but propitiate me from your royal largess!   90

                    A prisoner of the stars!
If only I could be on a queen's head again, Oríon
     Could shine up to Aquarius for all that I care.

Iambics

Hippónax redivivus here!
A dime will buy a longhorn steer
Where I have been. Iambic verse
Is still my forte, but this won't curse
Poor Búpalos or my old foes: 5
I'll tell you what a dead man knows.

[. . .]

Apollo, what a crowd of dead!
Like flies around a goatherd's head,
Or wasps that at a Delphic feast
Swarm around the butcher-priest;   10
Hekate, what fine cadavers
For Kharon's drooling, long palavers
As he poles them in his boat,
Shivering in his threadbare coat.
But silence now; write down my tale.   15
    One Báthykles—now don't grow pale,
I won't drag this on and on;
I must whirl back to Ákheron—
One Báthykles, an Arkadian,
Had all the things God gives a man . . .   20

[. . .]

He set the spindles here and there
With ribbons through them. Maidens were
Standing by to start them spinning . . .

[. . .]

So Thýrion, son of Báthykles,
Sailed to Milétos to find Thales,   25
A man of winning reputation
For general wit and education
And who mapped out the constellation
The Lesser Wain, those starry pips
Phoenicians use to steer their ships.   30
Our prelunar friend by good luck found

The hoary sage on holy ground,
Precinct of Apollo Dídymos,
Inscribing there what old Euphórbos,
The reincarnated Phrygian   35
Who lived in Pythagorean skin,
First discovered: scalene trines
And heptagrammic inscribed lines . . .

Hekálê

[. . .]
. . . sword thrust, and waved his club.
They all shrank back and dared not

look at the huge man and the monstrous beast
until Theseus shouted to them from far off:

"Be brave and wait. Let the swiftest messenger   5
run to town and tell my father, Aîgeus—

who will make it worth his while—this:
'Theseus is near by, leading the live bull

from watery Marathon.'" He spoke, and hearing him
they cried out Ἰή ΠΑΙΕΟΝ and stood firm.   10

The South Wind does not rain such a flood of leaves
nor the North Wind even in the leaf shedding month

as the countrymen then threw over Theseus;
standing in a circle around him the women

crowned him with sashes [15

[22 *lines missing*]

". . . and then when [   ] each
son of Oûranos constructed my wings, Pallas

left Hephaîstos's child locked in a chest a long time,
until the daughters of Kekrops [

secret, unspeakable, I knew not nor learned whose   20
child he was, but a rumor circulated among primal

birds that in truth Earth bore him to Hephaîstos.
Then Pallas, to build a bulwark for her land

newly seized by vote of Zeus and the other twelve
gods and through the serpent's witness, was going   25

to Pellénê in Akhaîa. Meanwhile the daughters
guarding the chest planned a wicked deed.
                    ] and picked the locks

[22 *lines missing*]

                    ] of Athena
          ] crows alone [30
by gods. Not I, Lady, when your heart
          ] of so much ill omen never [

nimble birds, then I helped [
And so she spurned our race, nor [

our [   ] heard [   ] but may you never fall   35
from her heart—Athena's anger weighs forever.

But I was there as a young crow; this is my
eighth generation, but my parents' tenth.

[11 *lines missing*]

I might have remedies from the belly's evil hunger,
but Hekálê [   ] supplicant [40

and barley groats dripped from the potion to earth
          ] this will be [
          ] bringing bad news. Would that you might be
still living at this time, so you might know

how the Thríai inspire an old crow. Yes by my—   45
not every day, you know—by my shriveled

old skin, yes by this tree, dry as it is—
"the chariot's pole and axle are not broken yet,

there's many a sunset still to come,"
but it will be evening, night, noon, or dawn,   50

when the crow, who now might even rival swans
or milk in color, or foam on a wave,

will put on deadly feathers, pitch black,
the pay Phoîbos will give for foul news

when he hears about the daughter of Phlégyas,   55
Korónis, who ran off with Ischys, a horsedriver."

She nodded off as she spoke, and her listener too,
into a sound but brief sleep. Frosty dawn

came early, the time when thieves' hands cease
pilfering, for the morning lamps shine,   60

the watercarrier sings his wellsong, the axle
creaks under the wagon and wakens the man

with a house by the road, and the blacksmith's slaves,
deaf themselves, torment the ear with incessant . . .

Lyrics

BRANKHOS

Gods most celebrated in song, Phoîbos and Zeus,
                    founders of Dídyma,

[. . .]

       ] let cursed, rapacious plague not strike
                    your animals,
       ] thrice dear to me, let it turn away   5
          ] may graze the green pasture
          ] take care of this; you and
                    those of your grandfathers
       ] to accompany [   ] It is true
       ] your father descended from Daîtes,   10
                    your mother's side
       ] Lápithes [   ] nobility.

Phoîbos, you spoke and his heart danced
       ] a lovely sanctuary in the woods
                    where you were first seen,   15
       ] near the double fountain planted
                    a sprig of bay.
Rejoice, Lord Delphinios; I began with your name
because you rode from Delos to Oîkos on a dolphin
he honors [   ] then back again to another   20
    ] Dídyma [   ] fragrant temple of Olympos
          ] lover [   ] Phoîbos
          holy family of lords
          ] will have
          ] star   25

[
[

          ] song

THE DEIFICATION OF ARSÍNOË

Let the god lead, without them I cannot sing.
                    ] to go ahead, Apollo

                                        ] I could
                                        ] walk after his hand.
Bride, already you are below the starry Wagon   5
                              ] stolen, running beyond the moon
                                    ] intense laments
                                    ] this one voice
                              ] our queen is gone.
                              ] after what suffering was she quenched?   10
                                    ] overflowing grief taught
                                    ] noble husband for his wife
                                    ] an offering to kindle the fire
                                    ] slender water
                              ] across from the altar of Thetis   15
                                    ] Thebes

[
you and I [
                                    ] endurable

[
                                    ] courage

[
[
                                    ] the bride   20
                                    ] shroud

[
[
by the mouth which [

[5 lines missing]

                                    ] another city will build
                                    ] brings to the sea
                                    ] holy [25
                                    ] the scales [
                                    ] elegancies [

And so the true report was brought to Proteus.

But she noticed smoke, the pyre's signal,
whirling thick, the winds in pursuit   30

[. . .]

and up the midsurface of the Thracian sea.
Philótera had just left Sicilian Enna
and was walking in the hills of Lemnos
away from Deo. She had not heard of your death,
O god-stolen, and she said [35
"Kharis, look out from the top of Mount Athos
to see clearly if the fires from the plain [
who has perished, what city glows in full flame?
I am afraid, fly away, the South Wind [
the clearing wind. Is my Libya in danger?"   40
the goddess said. When Kharis alighted on the snowy
mountain, said to be nearest the Bear star,
she gazed toward the famous coast of Pharos.
Forlorn, she cried out [
"Yes, yes a great evil [45
which carries fiery smoke from your city."
She said this [
"Where in my city [
they cut off [   ] to the dear [
husband went for his father-in-law [50
and I heard of the long-lived people [
until Lame-Foot [
the god ran; immediately [
will come to the house." She [
was not visible. Kharis spoke sad words: 55
"Don't weep for my land, your Pharos hasn't burned
to ashes; nor [
other news, not good, came to my ears.
Dirges in your city [
not for a commoner [60
the earth; but for one of the great [
They weep over the death of your only sister.
Whenever you look, the cities of the land
will be cloaked in black. Our rule . . .

THE ALL-NIGHT FESTIVAL

Apollo is in the chorus, I hear his lyre,
sense the Erótes and Aphrodite herself.

[. . .]

sweetheart [   ] join the all-night dance.
Stay awake until the crown of night,
seize the roasted honey cake, kottabos   5
prize, and kiss any girl, any boy you like.
O Kastor [   ] and you, Polydeûkes,
[   ] and [   ] of guests . . .

NOTES

HYMNS

Hymn I: To Zeus

After announcing his theme in the first line, the poet settles the rival claims of Arkadia and Crete to be the birthplace of Zeus—in favor of Arkadia. Zeus's birth in Arkadia is followed by his upbringing in Crete, rapid maturity, and accession to power. As ruler of the universe, Zeus takes a special interest in his human counterparts—kings—and has lavished special attention on the poet's own monarch. The poem closes with a prayer for prosperity and virtue.

1   Zeus's libations: This briefly suggests a dramatic scene. We are at a symposium, and libations to Zeus are being poured. The poet breaks into song.

3   Sons of Earth: The Giants, offspring of Ge, the Earth.

4   Diktaian, Lykaian: Dikte and Lykaion are mountains in Crete and Arkadia respectively.

7   Ida: Another mountain in Crete.

10   Cretans are always liars: C. is quoting Epimenides of Crete, the ultimate source of the Liar's Paradox.

11   Cretan-forged tomb: There were several "tombs of Zeus" in Crete, where he was originally regarded as a local hero and later deified.

13   Parrhasia: A mountainous region in Arkadia.

16   Eileithyia: Goddess of birth.

22–34   Ladon ... Eurymanthos ... Iaon ... Melas ... Karneion ... Krathis. . . Metope: rivers in Arkadia.

42ff.   Neda: In Hesiod's *Theogony* (361ff.) Neda is a daughter of Okeanos, born after Styx and Philyra. Here she is one of the nymphs who assisted at Zeus's birth. The river Neda rises in Mount Lykaion and flows westward into the Ionian Sea near the coastal town of Lepreion. The geographer Strabo says it rose from a spring created by Rheia to wash the infant Zeus.

49   Kaukonian: Descended from Kaukon, son of Lykaon, an Arkadian king.

53   Nereus: The sea.

57   Sons of the Bear: The Arkadians, descendants of Arkas (= Bear), the son of Zeus and Lykaon's daughter Kallisto, who was changed into a bear.

61   Thenai-by-Knossos: There were two Thenai—one in Arkadia, the other a small town near Knossos in Crete.

64   Umbilical plain: A literal translation of the Greek *omphalion pedon*, a place name that originally may have signified some kind of regional centrality.

65   Kydonians: Kydonia was in northwestern Crete.

66   Korybants: (Male) semidivine beings, attendants of Rheia.

67   ash-nymphs: The Meliai, nymphs associated with ash trees; here consorts of the Korybants.
     Adrestaia: A sister of the Kuretes.

69   Amaltheia: The she-goat who suckled Zeus (and whose horn became the Cornucopia).

72   Kuretes: Like the Korybants, attendants of Rheia.

73   Kronos: Zeus's infanticidal father, who had already swallowed his brothers and sisters.

80   Old poets lie: Homer *Iliad* 15.187ff.; Pindar *Olympian Odes* 7.54ff.

105 Artemis Khiton: See Hymn III, ll. 16ff., for the *khiton* ("fringed tunic") Artemis wore as hunter.

116 Ptolemy Philadelphos: An intruded gloss (C. says simply "our monarch"). It is possible that Philadelphos's father, Ptolemy Soter, is meant, or that C. wanted his poem to last for more than one regnum, or that he avoided the proper name for reasons of poetic decorum. We have inserted the proper name for our own reasons of poetic decorum: it renders the encomium a little more wholehearted, a little less fulsome.

Hymn II: To Apollo

The poem opens with an epiphany of Apollo in his temple. The god makes his presence felt, and a chorus of boys begins to sing his praises as Archer, Poet, Prophet, Healer, Pastoral God, and Founder of Cities. The foundation of Kyrene (C.'s hometown) under Apollo's protection is recounted in a lyrical, personal style. Then the ritual cry HIE PAIEON is heard and its origin is explained. The poem concludes with a visitation by Envy and his dismissal by Apollo, a passage that has become a famous literary manifesto.

The dramatic setting, established by allusions, is a celebration of Apollo's Karneian festival at Kyrene, but this does not imply that the poem was written for public performance at a festival.

Frederick Williams's study (*Callimachus, Hymn to Apollo: A Commentary* [Oxford 1978]) is lucid and definitive.

5-6 Delian palm tree: Leto supported herself on a palm tree on Delos when she gave birth to Apollo (see Hymn IV, ll. 230ff.)

7   the swan: See Hymn IV, ll. 275ff., for the association of the swan with Apollo.

15   HEKAËRGOS: Epithet of Apollo meaning "working from afar," referring to archery.

25   Lykorean Phoibos: Lykoreia was a town on Mount Parnassos, above Delphi. Phoibos as an epithet of Apollo means "shining."

28   HIË PAIEON: See the note on lines 103–7.

29–31   The reference is to Niobe, whose six sons and six daughters were killed by Apollo and Artemis because she boasted that she was superior to their mother, Leto, who had only two children. Niobe was turned into stone and her face was seen in a rock formation on Mount Sipylos near Smyrna.

34   my monarch: Probably Ptolemy III Euergetes, but the poem cannot be accurately dated.

41   Lyktian: Lyktos, a town in Crete, was famous for archery (see Epigrams 35 and 43).

43   Pytho: Delphi.

47   Panacea: "All-healing."

55   Amphryssos: A river in Thessaly.
Admetos: King of Pherai, in Thessaly. Zeus made Apollo serve Admetos as punishment for killing the Cyclopes.

64   Ortygian Delos: Ortygia, from the Greek word meaning "quail," was another name for Delos.

66   Kynthian goats: Kynthos was a mountain on Delos. See Epigram 43 for more Kynthian goats.

70   The Horn Altar at Delos was one of the Seven Wonders of the World.

71   Battos: Aristoteles of Thera, founder of the city of Kyrene in Libya. He assumed the name Battos (a native Libyan word meaning "king"), which then became the name of the royal house, of which C. was a member.

72   raven: Ravens were associated with Apollo, and according to Aristotle were able to distinguish fertile land from barren.

76   Boëdromios: "Rescuer, champion."

77   Klarios: Klaros, near Kolophon in Asia Minor, was a cult center and oracle of Apollo.

79   Karneian: A cult title of Apollo popular in many Doric cities (such as Sparta, Thera, and Kyrene).

81   six generations from Oedipus: Theras, the founder of Thera, was descended from Oedipus six generations removed.

82   Asbystia: the Asbystai were a native Libyan people.

92–93   Dorians . . . Kyre . . . Aziris: The Dorian colonists from Thera spent six years at Aziris before finally moving to Kyrene. Kyre was a spring that issued at the Temple of Apollo in Kyrene. It is one of the two etymologies for the name of the city (the other being the nymph Kyrene).

94ff.   Kyrene: A nymph, daughter of Hypsios. Apollo found her wrestling with a lion near Mount Pelion and transported her to Libya. There she killed a lion that had been preying on the cattle of Eurypylos, a king of Libya, and so won the kingdom. The Hill of Myrtles is in Kyrene.

103 PAIEON HIË: *Paieon* was originally an epithet of Apollo as Healer. *Hië* is derived from the Greek verb meaning "to shoot."

109–16 Envy suggests that "the sea" is the model of excellence in poetry. Apollo does not deny this but contrasts the muddiness of the great Euphrates with the purity of droplets from a mountain spring. The literary equivalents are: The sea is Homer, whose poems are expansive, pure (the Greeks thought of the sea as essentially pure), and the source of all later poetry (as the sea was thought to be the source of all other waters). The Euphrates represents later traditional epic poetry, which in its long course has become murky and stale. Droplets from a spring represent Callimachean poetry—fresh, pure, and delicate. The passage should be compared with the Prologue to the *Aetia*.

114 Cult of the Bees . . . Deo: Deo is Demeter, whose priestesses were sometimes called *Melissai* ("Bees"). But C. is probably thinking also of real bees, whose fastidiousness in collecting only sweet and pure liquids was reported by Aristotle, and whose activity was often compared with the activity of poets.

Hymn III: To Artemis

At the beginning of the poem, Callimachus portrays Artemis as a child-goddess who explores her new powers and grows into a mature goddess by the conclusion. The first half, in which the young Artemis requests and receives gifts from Zeus, is the most playful, humorous, and developed part of the poem. The second half begins with the poet reaffirming that Artemis is the subject of his poem. He asks Artemis herself to be his Muse by telling him directly about her properties so that he can tell others with his song. As Callimachus continues to list her attributes, a picture emerges of a powerful and dangerous goddess.

11 Phoibos: Artemis's brother Apollo.

13 Cyclopes: In Hesiod's *Theogony*, the Cyclopes are one-eyed giants, sons of Earth named Brontes ("Thunderer"), Steropes ("Lightner"), and Arges ("Bright"), who make thunderbolts and are excellent craftsmen.

15 Light Bringer: An epithet of Artemis (*Phosphoros* in Greek). Two of her other titles are Khitone (goddess who wears the short hunting tunic) and Eileithyia (goddess who helps women in childbirth).

23 Amnisos: A river in Crete.

31 Moirai: The three Fates.

35 In some tales Artemis was born first and then helped her mother, Leto, deliver Apollo.

60 Kairatos: A river near Knossos, in Crete.

61 Tethys: The daughter of Heaven and Earth; also the sister and wife of Ocean.

64 Lipara: An island north of Sicily among a cluster of volcanic islands, an appropriate place for the metalworking Cyclopes.

70 Ossa: A mountain in northern Thessaly.

76 Aetna: A large volcanic mountain in northeastern Sicily. It erupted several times in antiquity.

89 The little girl is immortal but still naughty.

101 Cyclopes have hairless chests. A. H. Griffiths ("Six Passages in Callimachus and the Anthology," *Bulletin of the Institute of Classical Studies* 17 [1970]: 33–35) sees this as a picture of the volcanic mountaintops in Sicily, which rise treeless above heavy forestation.

110 Arkadia: The region in the center of the Peloponnese.

111 Mainalos: A mountain in southern Arkadia.

125 Parrhasia: A mountain range in the southwest corner of Arkadia.

127 Anauros: A river.

135 The third labor of Herakles was to bring that Keryneian deer to Mykenai alive.

137 Tityos: A Euboian giant, son of Earth, who assaulted Leto or Artemis. Usually Apollo or Zeus kills the giant; Callimachus's Artemis does it herself.

141 Haimos: A chain of mountains forming the northern boundary of Thrace.

142 Boreas: The North Wind and a wind god.

146 Mysia: A district of northwest Asia Minor.

170 At the midpoint of the poem, Callimachus closes the first half with a prayer for Artemis's favor and begins the second half with his promise to sing about Artemis.

182 "Anvil of Tiryns": Herakles settled in Tiryns, a town of Argos.

201 Phrygia: A hill in Trakhis where Herakles was burned and immortalized.

204 Herakles killed and ate one of the oxen of Theiodamas, king of the Dryopes.

213 Artemis is no longer a child, but a popular young woman.

216 Inopos: A river in Delos which was thought to have a subterranean passage to the Nile.

217 Pitane and Limnai: Places in Lakonia with temples of Artemis.

219 Alai Araphenides: An Attic deme between Marathon and Brauron.

220   Skythia: A district north of Thrace, by the Black Sea. The Tauri worshipped Artemis with human sacrifice.

232   Helios, the sun, stops to watch the nymphs dance and thus makes the oxen work a long day if they were rented out.

241   Perge: A city of Pamphylia, on the river Kestros, in southern Asia Minor.

242   Taÿgeton: A mountain in Lakonia. Euripos: A harbor between Euboia and the mainland.

244   Gortyn: An important city on the south-central plain of Crete.

245   Britomartis: Originally a mother goddess of eastern Crete, and then identified with Diktyna, a similar goddess of western Crete. The goddess was later identified as Artemis herself or her attendant. *Diktyon* is the Greek word for "fishing net."

252   A tempting translation would be: "landed safe in the thick tuna nets—whence her name Diktyna."

263   Oupis: Another name for Artemis; C. is making an etymological play on "Oupis" (*Oupi*) and "shining-eyed" (*eu-opi*).

265   Kyrene: Apollo saw Kyrene wrestling with a lion by the Iolkion tomb of Pelias, near Mount Pelion. Awed by her strength and beauty, Apollo took her to Libya, where she founded the city of Kyrene. See Pindar's *Pythian Odes* 9.

268   The wife of Kephalos was Prokris, whom Kephalos killed by mistake when he was hunting.

271   Antikleia: Callimachus portrays Kyrene, Prokris, and Antikleia as Artemis's Amazon companions. Antikleia was also the daughter of Autolykus and the mother of Odysseus.

274   Atalanta: She was the daughter of Klymene and rejected marriage until she lost a foot race through trickery. A renowned hunter, Atalanta helped kill the Kalydonian boar that Artemis sent to ravage the kingdom of Kalydon in Aitolia.

281   Atalanta shot the centaurs when they insulted her.

287   Miletos: A city of Asia Minor, south of Ephesos, at the mouth of the Maeander River.

288   Neleus, son of Kodros, founded Miletos.

290   Khesion . . . Imbrasia: A cape and a river of Samos; an island northwest of Miletos.

296   Rhamnusian Helen: Helen is a daughter of Nemesis, who was worshiped at Rhamnos, in Attica.

297   Proitos: King of the district of Argos. His daughters insulted the statue of Hera or refused the Dionysian rites. Driven mad by the offended deity, they killed their children and wandered the countryside.

300   Azanian: Azania was another name for Arkadia, the land of Zeus (Zan).

301 Lusa is in Arkadia.

305 Amazons: A legendary race of female warriors. Hippo, also known as Hippolyte, was the Queen of the Amazons.

307 Ephesos: A city at the mouth of the Kayster River on the west coast of Asia Minor. Ephesos defended itself against the Kimmerians and Lydians until the Lydians eventually captured it and helped build the famous temple of Artemis there.

315 Sardis: A city northeast of Ephesos.

316 Berekynthians: A Phrygian people.

320–23 Pytho: Another name for Delphi; named for the great snake that Apollo killed in order to take over the site.

Lygdamis: King of the Kimmerians, who burned the temple of Artemis in 670 B.C.E. The Kimmerians lived north of the Black Sea until they were driven out by the Skyths. The Kimmerians overthrew Phrygia under the last king, Midas, and terrorized Ionia until they were gradually destroyed by wars with Lydia and Assyria. The Bosporos is the strait connecting the Black Sea and the Marmara Sea, named after Io, whom Zeus turned into a cow after raping her (bos = "cow" and poros = "passage").

328 Munikhia: A citadel on a steep hill on the eastern side of Piraeus overlooking the two harbors of Athens.

329 Pherai: A city of Thessaly on a hill overlooking a fertile district near the southern verge of the Pelasgiotis Plain.

331 Oineus: The king of Kalydon, who neglected to make sacrifices to Artemis.

334 Agamemnon was the son of Atreus. He shot a stag sacred to Artemis and boasted about it, which led to the sacrifice of his daughter Iphigenia.

Hymn IV: To Delos

Delos is the longest of the six hymns (326 lines in the Greek). The political references indicate that the poem was written in 270 B.C.E. In this poem, Callimachus sings the tale of the legends and cults of Delos, particularly of how Leto came to give birth to Apollo on Delos. By addressing the island of Delos as a woman, Callimachus emphasizes the similarities of Delos and Leto. The two are in constant motion, running and swimming, until they find each other and can rest at last. Delos originally fled into the sea to avoid Zeus, and presumably she keeps moving to continue to resist him. Hera denies Leto a place to give birth because Zeus had impregnated Leto. Finally, Delos and Leto are connected by virtue of being Apollo's nurse and mother.

8 Pimpleia: A fountain in Pieria, near Mount Olympos, that was sacred to the Muses.

11   Kynthos: Mountain on Delos where Leto gave birth to Apollo.
19   Tethys: Daughter of Earth and Heaven; sister and wife of Ocean.
22   island: Cyprus, named after Aphrodite (Kypris).
34   great god: Poseidon.
35   Telkhines: Semidivine beings on Rhodes who were skilled in metal working and magic. See the notes to the Prologue to the *Aetia*.
41   Asteria, which means "star," was the daughter of Titans. In order to escape from Zeus, she turned into a quail and threw herself from the sky, like a falling star, into the sea.
45   Saronic Gulf: The gulf of Athens.
46   Troëzen, named after the son of Pelops, was on the southern coast of Argos.
47   Ephyra: The ancient name for Kority, located in the Peloponnese at the junction of the mainland.
48   Euripos: The strait between Euboia and the mainland.
52   Khios: Khios and Samos are islands off the coast of Asia Minor. *Parthenia* means "maiden."
54   Mykale: A city on the mainland of Asia Minor, opposite Samos.
56   Delos was no longer unseen (*a-delos*) drifting on the sea.
65   Haimos: A chain of mountains forming the northern boundary of Thrace.
67   Seven caverns of Wind: The cave of Boreas, the North Wind. Iris, the daughter of Thaumas, was a personification of the rainbow and a messenger of the gods, especially Hera and Zeus.
68   Mimas: A mountain on the mainland opposite Khios.
71   Arkadia: A district in the center of the Peloponnese.
72–73   Parthenion and Pheneios were located in Arkadia.
79   father: The Ismenos River.
80   Asopos: A river in southern Boiotia, south of Thebes.
86   Helikon: The largest mountain (5,868 ft.) of Boiotia; a sanctuary of the Muses and the place where they greeted Hesiod.
99–104   Pytho: Another name for Delphi, an oracular site on Mount Parnassos near the Pleistos River, named after the snake goddess Apollo killed in order to take over her site. The priestess used laurel to inspire prophecies.
108   Theban woman: Niobe; she had twelve children, all of whom were killed by Artemis and Apollo when Niobe boasted of the quantity of her children in comparison to Leto's two. See Hymn II, ll. 29ff.
109   Kithairon: A mountain near Thebes.
112   Akhaia: The northernmost district of the Peloponnese.
115   Anauros: A river in Thessaly.
116   Larisa: A city of Thessaly on the Tempe River.

Kheiron: The son of Philyra and Kronos, this wise centaur lived on Mount Pelion, in Thessaly.

147   Eileithyia: The goddess who assisted women in childbirth; often identified with Artemis. In some stories, Leto bore Artemis first and Artemis helped Leto deliver Apollo.

149   Pangaion: A mountain in southern Thrace.

152   Ossa: A mountain on the northern coast of Thessaly.

153   Krannon: A plain near the Tempe River.
      Pindos: A mountain to the west of Krannon.

156   Aetna: A large volcano (10,758 ft.) in northeastern Sicily which erupted several times in antiquity.

169   Ekhinades: Islands at the mouth of the Akheloös River which bordered the districts of Akarnania and Aitolia.

170   Kerkyra: The large island in the Ionian Sea called Korfu today.

174   Kos: An island off the coast of the district of Karia in Asia Minor.

175   Merops, whose name means "articulate" or "bee-eater," was the mythical king and seer of Kos.

176   Khalkiope: The daughter of Eurypylos, a later king of Kos; she bore Thessalos by Herakles.

183   Saviors: The title of the Ptolemys. The unborn Apollo foresees the birth of Ptolemy II Philadelphos, son of Ptolemy I and Berenike, on Kos in 310–309 B.C.E.
      This political reference is to the invasion of Greece by the Gauls in 280–279. They attacked Delphi, but were routed. Some Gallic mercenaries revolted against Ptolemy II, who defeated them on the Nile.

194   According to *POxy.* 2225, two lines are missing after this line, and the next two lines are incomplete.

219   There are two garbled lines after this in the Greek text.

227   Inopos: A river in Delos which was thought to have a subterranean passage to the Nile.

276   Maionian Paktolos: A river by the city of Sardis of central Lydia in Asia Minor, which was thought to bear gold.

295   hard to plow: A physical description of Delos's rocky soil, but also a sexual reference to Delos's refusal to yield to Zeus's "plowing." Delos stops running in order to be Apollo's wet nurse.

297   Kerkhnis: A harbor of Corinth.

298   Lekhaeon: A second harbor of Corinth.
      Kyllene: A mountain in Arkadia.

302–4   The island of Delos was free of war and death; no one was buried there.

311   Pelasgians: The name used by Greeks for the pre-Hellenic people of Greece.
      Dodona: The seat of the most ancient Greek sanctuaries with an

oracle of Zeus, located in Epiros across from the island of Kerkyra. Zeus gave his oracles through the rustling of the wind in an oak tree; bronze vessels were sometimes hung in the tree.

317 Lelantian plain: In Boiotia.

319 Arimaspians: A legendary people of northeastern Skythia.

326–28 The Delian girls' offering was to their female ancestors; the Delian boys' offering was to their male ancestors.

333 Olen: A prehistoric poet who wrote about the Arismaspians.

340 Pasiphaë, wife of King Minos of Crete, bore a daughter, Ariadne, and a "monstrous son," Minotaur. Athens regularly sent fourteen youths as an offering to the Minotaur. Theseus, son of King Aegeus of Athens, sailed to Crete with the youths in the Sacred Ship. In Crete, guided by Ariadne, Theseus killed the Minotaur.

354 to her whom Leto bore: Artemis, who is not mentioned in the rest of the poem, although she is Apollo's twin.

Hymn V: The Bath of Pallas

The ancient rite in *The Bath of Pallas* refers to the Argive cult that centered on the annual ritual bathing of a wooden statue of Pallas Athena, the Palladium, and the shield of Diomedes. Diomedes, king of Argos, helped Odysseus steal the statue from Troy. Eumedes, a priest of Athena, fled from Argos with the statue and set it up on Kreion. Images of the Palladium and Athena mingle in the hymn.

The temple was dedicated to Athena Oxyderkes, which means "sharp-eyed," or "producing sharpness of sight." Callimachus put together an Argive cult with a Theban tale in order to emphasize the meanings of *vision.* No mortal can see a goddess naked and live unchanged. Athena takes Tiresias's eyesight but gives him the inner vision of the prophet in exchange. Throughout the poem Callimachus refers to eyes. He probably invented the version in which Aktaion saw Artemis bathing in order to make the two stories parallel.

For a detailed analysis see K. J. McKay, *The Poet at Play: Kallimachos, The Bath of Pallas* (Leiden, 1962).

The Bath of Pallas is one of the two hymns written by Callimachus in Doric dialect, and the only one written in elegiac couplets.

7 Pelasgian: The Greek name for the mythical pre-Hellenic people of Greece.

15 Akhaia: The northern district of the Peloponnese.

21 Paris, a Trojan prince, judged the beauty contest between Athena, Hera, and Aphrodite (Kypris); by his choice he began the Trojan War.

23 Simöis: A river near Troy in the district of Mysia in Asia Minor.

28 The "twin stars" were the Dioscuri—Kastor and Polydeukes—

sons of Tyndareos and Leda; brothers of Helen, who was Aphrodite's reward to Paris.

33–36   Athena is manly. After exhibiting her martial prowess, she cares for her horses and then takes a simple bath. Her toilet is like that of male athletes: she oils her body and hair.

42   Inakhos: The river, by the city of Argos, where the ritual bathing took place.

56   Physadeia: A spring in Argos.

57   Amymone: A spring in Argos; named after a daughter of Danaos who was raped by Poseidon at Argos. The word *amymon* in Greek means "blameless."

76   Thespiai: The chief city of southern Boiotia, near the eastern foot of Mount Helikon.

77   Plataia: A city in southern Boiotia between Mount Kithairon and the Asopos River.
     Haliartos: Also a city in Boiotia.

79   Koroneia: A city in Boiotia.

88   Helikon: The largest mountain of Boiotia; a sanctuary of the Muses.

101   Athena gave Diomedes the ability to see clearly so that he could distinguish between gods and men (Homer *Iliad* 5.127ff.) Here, Athena blinds Tiresias because he saw her naked. Athena Oxyderkes rewards or punishes according to her own nature. In an earlier version of how Tiresias became blind, Athena scratches out his eyes. Callimachus hints at that version.

116   roe: Roe deer (*dorkas*), named for its large eyes.

128   Moirai: The three Fates.

131–39   Athena tells the story of a future event: Aktaion, grandson of Kadmos, will see Artemis naked. Artemis will change Aktaion into a deer, and his own hounds will kill him.

149   Kadmos: The founder and first king of Thebes. He had four daughters, including Autonoe, and a son, Polydoros.

150   Labdakos: The son of Polydoros and the grandfather of Oedipus.

154   Agesilaos: "Leader of the people," an epithet of Hades, ruler of the underworld.

Hymn VI: To Demeter

The ritual framework for this hymn is a festival of Demeter, modeled upon the Athenian Thesmophoria, in which the women celebrants lead in procession a basket with mystic contents to the goddess's shrine. The festival becomes the occasion to recount a myth, and the poet, instead of dwelling on the sorrowful tale of Demeter's search for her daughter, tells the story of Erysikhthon, who by his sacrilegious greed brought down upon himself Demeter's curse. She afflicted him with a monumental hunger that he could never satisfy.

Hymn VI, like Hymn V, is written in Doric, and K. J. McKay sees in it elements of Doric comedy (*Erysikhthon: A Callimachean Comedy* [Leiden, 1962]).

7   Hesperos: The Evening Star.
8   Deo: Demeter.
9   ravaged daughter: Persephone.
11 the black men: The Ethiopians.
    gloomgolden apples: The apples in the garden of the Hesperides.
14 Akheloös: A river in northwestern Greece.
15 Kallikhoros: The sacred well at Eleusis.
22 Triptolemos: Son of Keleus, king of Eleusis.
24 son of Triopas: Erysikhthon.
25 Pelasgians: The pre-Hellenic inhabitants of Greece, originally a northern Aegean people uprooted by Bronze Age migrations.
    Old Thessaly: The original reads: "not yet in the Knidian land [Karia in Asia Minor] but still in holy Dotion [in Thessaly]."
30 Eleusis: Just west of Athens, site of the Eleusinian mysteries, the major cult of Demeter.
31 Triopa: Cult center of Demeter in Karia.
    Enna: Cult center of Demeter in Sicily.
42 Nikippe: Otherwise unknown.
75 Ormenos: Eponymous king of Ormenion in Thessaly.
76 Athena's Itonian Games: Athena had a cult at Itone in Thessaly.
78 Krannon: Mountain in Thessaly.
79 Polyxo . . . Aktorian: Otherwise unknown.
98 Kanake: Daughter of Aiolos.
106 Hestia: Goddess of the hearth.
126 Prytaneion: The town hall.

EPIGRAMS

Callimachus's epigrams have not survived in their own manuscript tradition. It is not even certain that Callimachus collected his epigrams for publication, but in one form or another they were widely circulated in antiquity. Meleager included a number of Callimachus's epigrams in his *Garland* (c. 80 B.C.E.), characterizing him in the prologue as "sweet myrtle brimming with bitter honey." About sixty epigrams by Callimachus are found scattered through the *Palatine Anthology*, the great Byzantine collection of Greek epigrams, and a few more are preserved in other sources.

In 1577 Nicodemus Frischlin published twenty-five epigrams of Callimachus from the *Planudean Anthology* (another Byzantine collection).

As scholars recovered more of Callimachus's epigrams from the *Palatine Anthology* (which emerged from obscurity in 1604), they added them in no particular order to Frischlin's collection. The resulting melange became the accepted order for the epigrams in such standard editions of Callimachus as Pfeiffer's and Mair's. A. S. F. Gow and D. L. Page (*Hellenistic Epigrams* [Cambridge, 1965]) rearranged the epigrams into categories derived from the *Palatine Anthology:* erotic, sepulchral, dedicatory, and epideictic. This is a rational system and we have adopted our own variation of it here: sepulchral (1–27), dedicatory (28–44), erotic (45–58), and literary (59–64).

The first two categories correspond to the original forms and purposes of epigram: verse inscriptions on tombstones and votive offerings. The terseness and control that such inscriptions require established the epigram as an art form that eventually replaced the personal lyric and appropriated its themes. Hence the erotic epigrams in the third group. The epigrams in the fourth group, on literary themes, are the natural product of an author with Callimachus's interests and critical disposition. They belong to a large class of Hellenistic and later Greek epigrams known as "epideictic"—displays of wit and technical expertise on famous people and works of art and literature.

The following notes identify the source of each epigram—usually the *Palatine Anthology*—and give the corresponding number of each epigram in G. R. Mair's Loeb Library edition.

I

Pal. Anth. 7.520; Mair 2. On Herakleitos of Halikarnassos, an elegiac poet, not to be confused (as he apparently is in the *Palatine Anthology*) with the philosopher Herakleitos of Ephesos. His poems may have borne the title *Nightingales.* Only one survives, an eight-line epitaph on a woman of Knidos (*Pal. Anth.* 7.465).

Of Callimachus's epigrams this is probably the best known (if not the only one known) to English readers, through W. Cory's translation:

> They told me Heraclitus, they told me you were dead,
> They brought me bitter news to bear, and bitter tears to shed [etc.].

2

Pal. Anth. 7.522; Mair 17. An epitaph in the dramatic form of a passer-by reading an inscription. Actual inscriptions in a similar form have survived. The principals are unknown. There were two cities called Methymna: one on Lesobs, the other in western Crete.

3

Pal. Anth. 7.519; Mair 16. Kharmis cannot be identified. The poem is more an expression of condolence than an epitaph. There is some scholarly debate about whether "the morning demon" should be personified.

4

Pal. Anth. 7.277; Mair 59. Leontikhos is unknown. For the comparison of the melancholy sailor with a gull, C. may be indebted to Aratos *Phainomena* 296ff.:

> But like flashing gulls that dive for their food
> We sit amid ship staring at shoreline and sea
> While the waves beat the beach ever farther away
> And a thin piece of timber protects us from death.

5

Pal. Anth. 7.517; Mair 22. The principals are unknown, although the Greek text gives the family name (Aristippos) and the town (Kyrene). The comparison between dawn and a black horse is suggested in the Greek by the juxtaposition of the word for dawn and the name Melanippos ("black horse").

6

Pal. Anth. 7.459; Mair 18. Krethis is unknown and the name is otherwise unattested. Samos is an island off the coast of Asia Minor, but the epitaph may have been written for Samians living in Alexandria.

7

Pal. Anth. 7.728; Mair 41. The Kabiri were the gods of Samothrace, but their cult was widespread. They were primarily marine deities, protectors of seafarers (see Epigram 37). Kybele is the Great Mother, whose cult originated in Phrygia and spread throughout the Hellenistic and Roman worlds.

8

Pal. Anth. 7.271; Mair 19. Inscription for a cenotaph. The principals are unknown. See Epigraph 27 for another cenotaphic inscription with a different tone.

9

Pal. Anth. 7.458; Mair 51. "Mikkos" is a nursery name of the sort that sometimes sticks in adult life.

Pal. Anth. 7.460; Mair 28. "Mikylos," connected with *mikros,* has connotations of modesty and humility. The prayer that Earth and other chthonic powers rest lightly on the dead is fairly common in Greek epitaphs.

Pal. Anth. 7.520; Mair 12. It appears from 1.2 that Timarkhos was a philosopher, but very little is known about any of the possible candidates bearing that name.

Pal. Anth. 7.451; Mair 11. Neither Saon nor Dikon was a common name. There were five cities called Akanthos.

Pal. Anth. 7.521; Mair 14. Kyzikos, on the island of Arktonessos, was an important commercial town near the Propontis. The principals are unknown. Epitaphs appealing to passers-by to bring the news back home are a common type.

Pal. Anth. 7.523; Mair 61. Kimon and Hippaios are unknown. Elis is in the northwestern Peloponnese, near Olympia.

Pal. Anth. 7.453; Mair 21. Philip and Nikoteles cannot be identified. The point of the epigram, as translated here, is its quiet dignity and poignancy, not, as J. Ferguson maintains (*Callimachus* [Boston, 1980], p. 147), a play on the names *Philip* ("horse-lover") and *Nikoteles* ("victor").

Pal. Anth. 7.525; Mair 23. Epitaph for C.'s father, but concerned with his grandfather and himself; perhaps something of an apologia for his career as a poet. In the *Anthology* this epigram has two additional lines; they are identical to the last two lines of the Prologue to the *Aetia,* and scholars now agree they are interpolated from there.

Pal. Anth. 7.415; Mair 37. Epitaph for C., jesting in earnest. On Battos see Hymn II, l. 71, and note.

Pal. Anth. 7.724; Mair 57. Menekrates is unknown; Ainos was a thriving Greek city on the coast of Thrace. Centaurs were notorious for drunkenness. C. may have been thinking in particular of Homer, *Odyssey* 21.295: "Wine deranged also the famous Centaur Eurytion."

19

Plutarch, *Antony* 70; Mair 3. Timon of Athens, the famous misanthrope, was a favorite subject for fictitious epitaphs. He seems to have lived in the mid-fifth century B.C.E.

20

Pal. Anth. 7.318; Mair 4.

21

Pal. Anth. 7.317; Mair 5. The dead in Hades were the Great Majority.

22

Pal. Anth. 9.67 (where it is anonymous); Mair 8. Planudes attributes this epigram to C.

23

Pal. Anth. 7.447; Mair 13. Theris cannot be identified. The epigram is probably fictitious.

24

Pal. Anth. 7.524; Mair 15. This dialogue may express the views of either Callimachus or Kharidas (otherwise unknown, but presumably not fictitious since he is said to be from Kyrene, C.'s hometown) on the mythology of the underworld. The cheapness of things in Hades was proverbial; the last line translates a proverb that literally runs, "An ox of Pella [a small coin] will buy a great ox."

25

Pal. Anth. 7.518; Mair 24. Hardly intended as a serious epitaph, and here interpreted as a literary lampoon directed against an unfortunate poet, Astakides (otherwise unknown), who took up pastoral verse and attracted a following. Daphnis is the traditional hero of pastoral poetry. Dikte is a sacred mountain in Crete.

26

Pal. Anth. 7.471; Mair 24. Kleombrotos of Ambrakia (in northwestern mainland Greece) is unknown, although he may be the Kleombrotos mentioned in Plato's *Phaedo* (59C) as being away in Aigina at the time of Socrates' death. The *Phaedo* argues for the soul's immortality and the folly of fearing death, but specifically denounces suicide (61C).

Pal. Anth. 7.272; Mair 20. Lykos (whose name means "wolf") is unknown. Naxos is the largest of the Cyclades islands. Aigina is an island in the Saronic Gulf, south of Athens. The Goat Stars are the Haedi, Capella, and her Kids in the constellation Auriga. Their setting at dawn was a proverbial sign of storms (see Aratos *Phainomena* 679ff.). Ferguson (*Callimachus*, p. 148) points out the irony of the Kids' destroying the Wolf.

28

Athenaeus 7.318b; Mair 6. Dedication of a nautilus shell to Aphrodite (Kypris) at her temple on the peninsula of Zephyrion, where she was worshipped under the cult title of Arsinoë, wife of Ptolemy II Philadelphos. Iulis was the chief town on the island of Keos, where Selenaia (otherwise unknown) presumably found the shell. C.'s description of the nautilus seems to be drawn from Aristotle's account of the Argonaut, or Paper Nautilus (*Historia Animalium* 622b5). Smyrna, on the coast of Asia Minor, was originally an Aiolic colony. After a period of decline it was refounded by Alexander and became one of the great cities in the Hellenistic world.

Pal. Anth. 5.145; Mair 52. Inscription on a statute of Berenike, wife of Ptolemy III Euergetes (heroine of *The Rape of the Lock*). The statue has just been dedicated and annointed with perfume.

Pal. Anth. 6.150; Mair 58. Inscription for a statue dedicated to Isis.

Pal. Anth. 6.347; Mair 35. Phileratis is a name otherwise unattested.

Pal. Anth. 6.146; Mair 54. Dedication to Eileithyia, goddess of childbirth.

Pal. Anth. 6.148; Mair 56. Dedication of a lamp to Sarapis, the "God of Kanopos." Sarapis was an Egyptian god combining aspects of the bull Apis and the god Osiris. The god's temple at Alexandria, the Sarapeum, was one of the wonders of the ancient world.

Pal. Anth. 13.7; Mair 38. Menitas was probably a mercenary from Crete (Lyktos was in Crete). Hesperis was the westernmost town in the Kyrenaika; its name (which means "western") was changed to Berenike during the reign of Ptolemy III Euergetes. For Sarapis see the previous epigram.

Pal. Anth. 9.336; Mair 26. Inscription for a statue, or relief, of a cult hero. The typical representation would have had the warrior mounted on horseback carrying a sword or spear, with a snake in the scene to symbolize the hero's chthonic associations. A sculptor named Eëtion appears in an epigram by Theokritos (*Pal. Anth.* 6.337).

Pal. Anth. 13.25; Mair 40. Dedication by a merchant from Naukratis (an Egyptian port) at the temple of Demeter and Persephone at Thermopylai. Akrisios of Argos was the mythical (hence "Pelasgian") founder of the Amphictyonic Council, which met at Thermopylai.

Pal. Anth. 6.301; Mair 48. The original puns on the ambiguous sense of *hals* as "salt" and "sea." The epigram is a takeoff on dedicatory epigrams for thanks-offerings by sailors saved from storm at sea. The Gods of Samothrace are the Kabiri (Epigram 7).

Pal. Anth. 6.130; Mair 49. Simos is a schoolboy who has dedicated to the Muses a tragic mask of Dionysos. Glaukos's exchange of golden armor for Diomedes's brass (*Iliad* 6.236) was proverbial. The *Gaping God of Samos* was evidently a famous cult statue of Dionysos on Samos. "Sacred is the hair" is a line from Euripides' *Bacchae* (494) spoken by Dionysos when Pentheus threatens to cut the god's hair.

Pal. Anth. 6.311; Mair 50. Dedication of a comic mask celebrating a victory in a dramatic contest. Pamphilos is a typical character in New Comedy, the young man upon whose love affairs the plot hinges. Agoranax, the Rhodian playwright, is otherwise unknown.

Pal. Anth. 6.147; Mair 55. Inscription for a dedicatory plaque vowed by one Akeson (meaning "doctor," perhaps a significant name) to Asklepios, son of Apollo and god of healing, for curing his wife, Demodike.

Pal. Anth. 6.121; Mair 63. Inscription for a bow dedicated to Aretmis. Mount Kynthos is on Delos, birthplace of Apollo and Artemis, sacred ground and undoubtedly off-limits to hunters. Cretans were legendary archers, and Ekhemmas is represented as vying with Artemis, who hunts Kynthian goats in Hymn II, l. 66.

Pal. Anth. 6.351; Mair 36. To Herakles, slayer of the Nemean Lion and Erymanthian Boar. Arkhinos of Crete is unknown.

Pal. Anth. 6.149; Mair 57. Inscription for a bronze fighting cock dedicated to Kastor and Polydeukes, perhaps commemorating a victory in a cock fight but here interpreted as sexual innuendo. Euainetos and his forebears are unknown.

Pal. Anth. 13.24; Mair 39. Dedication of a prostitute's paraphernalia to Aphrodite. The note of resignation at the end is the translators' response to a hopelessly corrupt Greek text.

Pal. Anth. 12.103; Mair 33. Paraphrases of this epigram are found in Horace (*Sermones* 1.2.105–8) and Ovid (*Amores* 2.9.9).

Pal. Anth. 12.139; Mair 45.

47

Pal. Anth. 12.51; Mair 31. Akheloös, a river in northwestern Greece, was a poeticism for water in general.

48

Pal. Anth. 12.230; Mair 53. Quite possibly this Theokritos is the poet of the *Idylls*. Ganymede, son of Tros, was abducted by Zeus, posing as an eagle, and taken to Olympos to be the gods' cupbearer.

49

Pal. Anth. 12.118; Mair 43. The poet apologizes to his lover for serenading him, usually an unruly, friendly-aggressive act. This epigram was found inscribed on a wall in a first-century A.D. house on the Esquiline Hill in Rome. The Greek words for "rashness" and "self-restraint" may reflect the language of Stoic psychology.

50

Pal. Anth. 12.148; Mair 34. "Don't tell me my own dream": proverb for something one already knows all too well. See Epigram 38.

51

Pal. Anth. 12.71; Mair 32.

52

Pal. Anth. 12.149; Mair 46. Hermes is familiarly addressed as the bringer of good fortune, in this case a lover whom the poet has won by the risky ploy of telling him their incipient affair would never work out and then dismissing him.

53

Pal. Anth. 122.73; Mair 42. There is an imitation of this epigram by the Roman poet Q. Lutatius Catulus.

54

Pal. Anth. 5.6; Mair 27. The last two lines contain a reference, more specific in the Greek, to the Delphic oracle's response to the Megarians when they asked which city-states were the most powerful. The oracle concluded: "But you Megarians are not third or fourth or twelfth, or even on the list at all."

55

Pal. Anth. 12.134; Mair 44. The carnation falling from the lapel represents the roses falling from the wreath in the original Greek.

56

Pal. Anth. 12.150; Mair 47. In Theokritos's Idyll 2 the Cyclops Polyphemos solaces his love for Galatea with a song. Theokritos addressed that idyll to his friend Nikias, a physican. Philip, the addressee of this epigram, is un-known, but one suspects that he is parallel to Nikias and that this accounts for the medical terminology in the poem.

57

Pal. Anth. 5.23; Mair 64. A paraclausithyron, the complaint of a locked-out lover, a motif that became popular with the Roman elegiac poets. This is C.'s only heterosexual epigram. "Konopion" is a woman's name that means "gnat."

58

Pal. Anth. 12.43. A famous Callimachean manifesto, sometimes quoted without the erotic coda. The "handsome . . . has him" echo is in the origi-nal Greek.

59

Pal. Anth. 9.565; Mair 59. Theaitetos is known as an epigrammatic poet, contemporary with C. The point here is that he rejected dramatic poetry in favor of a purer form.

60

Pal. Anth. 9.566; Mair 10. Some take this and the following epigram as evi-dence that C. had a career as a dramatist. No trace remains, however, of any plays.

61

Pal. Anth. 9.362; Mair 60. Pylades (plural "Pyladae") of Phokis was Orestes' friend through thick and thin. The addressee, Leukaros, is unknown.

62

Pal. Anth. 9.507; Mair 29. Aratos of Soloi (in Asia Minor), C.'s contempo-rary, was the author of the *Phaenomena*, a didactic poem on astronomy. "Subtle" (*lepte*) is an important term in C.'s literary aesthetic, and a word that appears as an acrostic at *Phaenomena* 783–87.

Strabo 14.638; Mair 7. Strabo, the geographer, quotes this epigram in the course of his discussion of Samos. Kreophylos's poem, *The Taking of Oikhalia*, was the story of Herakles' revenge upon Eurytos, king of Oikhalia, after the latter refused to give Herakles his daughter Iole in marriage.

64

Pal. Anth. 7.89; Mair 1. In his life of Pittakos, Diogenes Laertius cites this poem as Callimachus's. The "flat and straightforward" style of the poem (Gow and Page's phrase), and the fact that it is listed as "anonymous" in the *Palatine Anthology*, have led some to condemn it as unauthentic. Its length is certainly unepigrammatic. But the theme is Callimachean: "Stay in your own lane." This theme may be placed alongside Apollo's advice to the poet in the Prologue in the *Aetia*.

Pittakos was one of the proverbial Seven Sages. Atarneus was on the coast of Asia Minor, just across from Mytilene on the island of Lesbos. Dion is a common name. As the addressee of this poem, Dion is unknown.

FRAGMENTS
Prologue to the Aetia

The most famous of Callimachus's poems were the *Aetia* and the *Hekale*. *Aetia* means "cause" or "origin." The *Aetia*, an elegiac poem in four books, is made up of a series of loosely connected explanations of legends, rites, and history. Callimachus produced an edition of his poetry which included the *Aetia*, *Iambi*, *Lyrics*, and *Hekale*. Only fragments of these poems exist today. The first and second books of the *Aetia* are dedicated to the Muses; the third and fourth, to Queen Berenike II, wife of Ptolemy III. Poems to Berenike frame the last two books: *The Victory of Berenike* begins the third book, and *The Lock of Berenike* ends the fourth book. We have translated five of the larger and more interesting fragments of the *Aetia*: the Prologue, Fragment 2, *The Victory of Berenike*, *Akontios and Kydippe*, and *The Lock of Berenike*.

C. seems to have added the Prologue to a revised edition of the *Aetia* published late in his life. It is a polemic against his critics and an apologia for his own style of poetry. Most of the text is known only through papyri; parts of lines, especially beginnings, are often missing. The translation here has stitched things together and offers a few reasonable conjectures as patches.

   1   gnomes . . . in Rhodes: A translation of the Greek word *Telkhines*. A race of gnome-like creatures inhabiting the island of

Rhodes, these metalworkers and sorcerers were often malicious. C. uses the term to refer to his critics. Rhodes was a center of literary activity and was for a while a haven for C.'s contemporary Apollonios, author of the *Argonautika* and later director of the Library at Alexandria. The details of a supposed literary feud (for which there is little or no evidence) between C. and Apollonios have been endlessly and fruitlessly debated.

10   *Demeter's Cornucopia:* A guess at the title of a (presumably interminable) poem by "fertile Demeter" alluded to in the text. Philitas of Kos wrote a *Demeter*, but his name is usually linked with C.'s as a stylistic model rather than opposed. The text is fragmentary here.

11–12   *Mimnermos . . . fat Lady poem:* Mimnermos (seventh century B.C.E.), of Kolophon and Smyrna, was a elegiac poet whose surviving poetry often has an attractive lyrical quality. His poems were collected in two books, one of which was called *Nanno* after a flute girl he loved. As a collection, the *Nanno* seems to have been a bulky miscellany of uneven appeal, hence (perhaps) "the fat Lady." But "Lady" is also a translator's pun on Antimachus's *Lyde*, a fourth-century epic and perhaps Callimachus's target here. The text is difficult.

12–15   The lines about cranes and pygmies and the Massagetai fighting the Medes are cited as examples of questionable taste in epic poetry, itself a questionable genre. For cranes and pygmies see Homer's *Iliad* 3.2ff. The Massagetai lived east of the Caspian Sea. They figured in Alexander's campaigns; the reference may be to some contemporary historical epic.

25ff.   Vergil translates these lines in *Eclogues* 6.3–5.

35–36   *Sicily . . . Enkelados:* Zeus imprisoned the Titan Enkelados under Mount Aetna in Sicily; Enkelados's restless heaving was considered the source of Aetna's volcanic activity.

Aetia

FRAGMENT 2   With his hoof Pegasos created the spring Hippokrene ("horse spring") on Mount Helikon. The poem, from Book I of the *Aetia*, is fragmentary after the first three lines. The quote in line 6 is an adaptation from Hesiod's *Works and Days* (625).

Victory of Berenike

Four new fragments of papyrus, containing sixty lines of Callimachus, were published by Claude Meillier in *Cahiers de recherches de l'institut de Papyrologie et d'Egyptologie de Lille* 4 (1976). The new fragments came from mummy cartonnage from excavations in Fayum, near ancient

Magdola, in 1901–1902. The writing dates from the late third century B.C.E.—within a generation of Callimachus's death. The new and the already existent fragments provide at least a diagram of the whole poem, which was probably around two hundred lines long. Berenike married in 247 B.C.E., which gives some indication of when the poem was written.

Two texts were invaluable to this translation and the notes: P. J. Parsons, "Callimachus: Victoria Berenices," *Zeitschrift für Papyrologie und Epigraphik* 25 (1977): 1–50; and *Supplementum Hellenisticum*, ed. Hugh Lloyd-Jones and Peter Parsons (Berlin, 1983), pp. 100–117.

F R A G M E N T   1   Sources: *P.Lille 76; P.Oxy.* 2173 (fr. 383 Pfeiffer). The first fragment describes the occasion of the song: news reached Egypt from Argos that Berenike's horses had won the chariot race in the Nemean Games held in honor of Zeus. The tapestry would be weavings dedicated to Hera in Argos commemorating Berenike's victory. Perhaps the tapestry pictured the story told in the rest of the poem: how Herakles killed the lion that Hera sent to ravage the valley of Nemea in Argos and established the Nemean Games. The reconstructions in this fragment are from Richard Thomas's "Callimachus, the Victoria Berenices, and Roman Poetry," *Classical Quarterly* 33, no. 1 (1983).

14   delicate weavings: Gk *leptaleos*; a hint linking the tapestry with Callimachus's poem.
15   bull: The Egyptian god Apis.

F R A G M E N T   2   *P.Lille* 76, 79. Herakles stays with an old peasant, Molorkhos, in Kleonai while preparing to kill the lion. The bulk of the lines have Herakles conversing with Molorkhos before he kills the lion (frs. 2–5). After he kills it, Herakles returns to Molorkhos to repeat Athena's instructions on establishing the Nemean Games (frs. 6–10).

19   Tanagra: The chief town of eastern Boiotia.
22   Taphian: Herakles' stepfather, Amphitryon, fought the Taphians.
30   wild pear: Prickly pear. Herakles wonders why the land is neglected. Molorkhos tells him that he cannot go outside his walls because of the lion.
49   Rheia: According to one tradition, the lion fell from the moon; according to another, Hera herself produced it. Perhaps the passage means that Rheia claimed to give birth to a stone, but the lion really is a stone that crushes Nemea.

F R A G M E N T   3   Source: Fr. 177 Pfeiffer. Molorkhos is the mouse-killing hero; the language equates the mice with the Nemean lion.

57   Ophion: The sun shines by night in the underworld, where the older gods live, the descendants of Ophion overthrown by Zeus.
74   tails: The Greek word, *alkaia*, is used of a lion's tail.

78 stone: Like the lion in fragment 2.
80 ravening beasts: A phrase used to describe lions.
84 double death: Poison and a spring mousetrap.

FRAGMENT 4 Source: Fr. 177 Pfeiffer.

FRAGMENT 5 Source: *P.Lille* 78a.
92 monsters: The lion. Herakles is still speaking to Molorkhos.
96 Melampos: A guest of Iphikles, whose impotence he cures, on
    his way to obtain cattle for his brother, Bias. Herakles says that
    if he succeeds in destroying the lion, then Molorkhos will be rich
    with cattle, like Melampos, because the lion will not keep
    depleting his stock. But if the lion eats Herakles, then Molorkhos
    should sacrifice an ox in Herakles' honor.

FRAGMENT 6 Source: Fr. 57 Pfeiffer. The missing portion before this fragment describes Herakles' victory and return to Molorkhos.
The unintentional irony of the first two lines (106–7) is that time has
indeed "cut away [the] song's length" and left a hefty part to our imagina-
tion.

FRAGMENT 7 Sources: Frs. 58 and 59 Pfeiffer. Herakles' narrative
ends in this fragment.
113 parsley crown: The crown awarded to winners in the Nemean
     Games.
113 pine: Formerly awarded to winners in the Isthmian Games held
     in honor of Poseidon near Corinth; now replaced by wild celery
     or parsley.
120 Ephyra: The name for ancient Corinth.
129 mule: Herakles returns to Molorkhos the mule that he bor-
     rowed.

FRAGMENT 8 Fr. 55 Pfeiffer.
135 wife: Argos was Hera's city, but she produced (vomited up) the
     lion even so.
137 bastard: Herakles.

FRAGMENT 9 Fr. 677 Pfeiffer.

FRAGMENT 10 Source: Fr. 597 Pfeiffer.

Akontios and Kydippe

Akontios from Keos fell in love with Kydippe from Naxos at an annual
festival for Artemis on Delos. Akontios carved the words "I swear by
Artemis to marry Akontios" on an apple and dropped it in Kydippe's path
as she entered Artemis's temple. When Kydippe read the inscription aloud,

she bound herself by the oath. Since Kydippe's father, Keyx, did not know of the oath, he betrothed her three times; each time Kydippe fell sick. Keyx asked Apollo for advice, learned the truth, and married Kydippe to Akontios.

Callimachus then moves from the story of Akontios and Kydippe to other legends of Keos that he had heard from the same source, the chronicler Xenomedes.

FRAGMENT 67

4   Iulis: A city of Keos, an island off the southern coast of Attika.

5   Euxantios: The son of Minos and Dexithea; some of his children settled in Keos.

6   Promethes: The son of Kodros, king of Attika; Promethes lived in Keos.

7   Kynthian: A name for Apollo because he was born on Mount Kynthos on Delos.

14   Ariadne: The daughter of Minos and Pasiphaë, rulers of Crete. She helped Theseus kill the Minotaur and escape from Crete to Naxos, where Theseus abandoned her. The god Dionysos fell in love with her on Naxos, where she was honored.

FRAGMENT 68

15   youth: Akontios.

FRAGMENT 69

19   Sicilian game: Called *kottabos* in Greek.

FRAGMENT 75

25–27   The night before her wedding, Kydippe should sleep with a boy whose "parents were alive" ("blooming on both sides" is the literal translation) for the ritual, but she falls sick that evening.

28   This line refers to the secret marriage of Zeus and Hera (*Iliad* 14.294.

31   rites: The Eleusinian mysteries.

49   Lygdamis: The king of the Kimmerians, who burned the temple of Artemis at Ephesos in 670 B.C.E.
Amyklaia: A town on Lakonia, about three miles south of Sparta; famous for its sanctuary of Apollo.

50   Parthenios: A river of Pontos; the word means "virgin."

55   electrum: An alloy of gold and silver.

57   Kodros: The last king of Athens in the eleventh century; his sons led the colonization of Ionia from Athens.

58   Aristaios: Kyrene and Apollo's son built an altar and established an annual sacrifice to Zeus Ikmios (meaning "moisture") when Keos suffered from diseases caused by the heat of the "Dog days"

of Sirius. Thenceforth, the winds blew for forty days after the rise of Sirius.

69 Iphikles: Well known for his speed.

71 Midas: A king of Phrygia who was famous for his wealth because everything he touched turned to gold.

76 Xenomedes: A Kean chronicler in about 450 B.C.E.

79 Parnassos: The mountain on which the oracular center of Delphi is located.

80 island: Keos, which was then called Hydrussa (meaning "watery").

81 Karians: The people of the district of Karia in Asia Minor. In prehistoric times the Karians and Leleges (another tribe) spread to the Aegean Islands.

83 Alalaxios: A war cry.

86 old man: Xenomedes.

87 Telkhines: Semidivine beings of Rhodes who were skilled in metalworking and magic.

89 Makelo: The daughter of Demonax; she was spared because she had entertained Zeus and Apollo.

90-91 The black magic of the Telkhines provoked the gods to destroy all the inhabitants of Keos except Makelo and her daughter, Dexithea, who married Minos and began Akontios's line.

98 Kean: Akontios.

The Lock of Berenike

This Berenike was the granddaughter of Ptolemy I's queen, Berenike I, and the wife of her cousin Ptolemy III Euergetes (who reigned from 247–222 B.C.E.). Soon after their marriage Ptolemy set out on an expedition against Syria. Berenike vowed a lock of her hair to the gods for her husband's safe return. The lock was duly deposited in the temple of the deified Arsinoë but disappeared under mysterious circumstances. Konon, the court astronomer, saved the day. Claiming that the lock had been translated into stars by divine agency, he proved his assertion by pointing to the hitherto unrecognized constellation now known as Coma Berenices.

The poem is a monologue spoken by the enstarred lock of hair. C. apparently wrote it as an independent piece of court poetry and later incorporated it into the *Aetia*. About a third of the Greek text survives on papyrus, but we have all of Catullus's translation of the poem into Latin verse (Catullus 66). Catullus's translation is very close in the passages that can be compared, and since there is no reason to suppose that it is not equally so throughout, we have translated Catullus's text here in its entirety.

1 Konon: Astronomer and mathematician from Samos who later settled in Alexandria. He was known for his research on solar

eclipses and was praised by Archimedes for his mathematics.

5 Latmos: Selene, the Moon-Goddess, used to meet her lover, En-
dymion, in a cave on Mount Latmos in Karia (in Asia Minor).

12 The expedition against Syria in 246 B.C.E. was undertaken to
avenge the murder of Antiokhos II, king of Syria and husband of
Ptolemy Euergetes' sister.

22 a cherished brother: Berenike was really Ptolemy's cousin, but in
the pharaonic tradition she was thought of as his sister. The
Greek word for *cousin* and *brother/sister* is the same.

43–45 The Persian king Xerxes, moving to invade Greece, cut a ship
canal through the Isthmus of Athos (Herodotos 7.24).

44 Thia: Hesiod (*Theogony* 371) says that Thia was the mother of
Helios.

48 Khalybes: A tribe of ironworkers in the Pontos.

52 Memnon's brother: Memnon, a son of Eos, the Dawn, had two
brothers: Zephyros, the West Wind; and Emathion, who was
associated with the ostrich. Both images are appropriate: Ari-
sonoë's epithet is Zephyritis, and according to Pausanias (9.31.1)
she (Z.) was sometimes represented riding an ostrich.

52–55 Arsinoë . . . Zephyritis: Arsinoë was the deified wife of Ptolemy
II Philadelphos. Her temple was on the Zephyrion Peninsula
(between Alexandria and Kanopos). See Epigram 28.

57 Ariadne's crown: The constellation Corona Borealis, which was
placed in the heavens by Dionysos in honor of his bride, Ariadne.

62–65 These lines accurately describe the position of Coma Berenices
relative to the other constellations. The constellation itself is
very dim, being a large, open cluster of fifth- and sixth-magnitude
stars, but it is a beautiful shimmering specter in a dark sky.

63 Kallisto, the Arkadian Bear: Daughter of Lykaon, the Arkadian,
she was banished from the company of Artemis after she was
made pregnant by Zeus. Hera turned her into a bear, and when
she was about to be killed by her son Arkas, Zeus translated her
into the constellation now known as Ursa Major.

64–65 Boötes: The Herdsman, with its bright star Arcturus, follows
Ursa Major across the sky. Boötes, being nearly a circumpolar
constellation in the latitude range of the Greek world, takes a
long time to set.

92–93 Orion and Aquarius are constellations in different parts of the
sky.

Iambics

Callimachus's book in iambic meter included thirteen poems; the translation presented here is from the first poem. Iambics were used primarily for
fable, invective, and satire.

1   Hipponax: A poet of Ephesos who wrote iambics in the sixth cen-
        tury B.C.E. His poems had a coarse and frank style. Here he rises
        from the dead (redivivus) to continue his lampoons on modern
        foes.
5   Bupalos: A sculptor and a victim of the historical Hipponax's
        poetry.
16   Bathykles: He sent his son, Amphalkes, to present a gold cup to
        the wisest man. Amphalkes gave it to Thales, a pre-Socratic
        philosopher, one of the Seven Sages, and a follower of Pythagoras.
        (Pythagoras believed himself to be a reincarnation of the Trojan
        Euphorbos.) Each of the Seven Sages passed on the cup to the
        next, until it came again to Thales, who dedicated it to Apollo.
18   Akheron: A river in the Akherusian plain at the confluence of
        the Kokytos and Pyriphlegethon streams; it was said to lead to
        Hades.
19   Arkadia: A region in the center of the Peloponnese.
25   Miletos: A city in southwestern Asia Minor.
31   prelunar: Arkadians were thought to be older than the moon.

Hekale

FRAGMENT 260 Sources: Fr. 260 Pfeiffer; *Supplementum Hellenisticum*, ed. Hugh Lloyd-Jones and Peter Parsons (Berlin, 1983), no. 288.
The *Hekale* was a long poem (perhaps 1,000 lines) with many digressions.
The primary myth is of Theseus taming the Bull of Marathon. Theseus
escaped from Medea and arrived in Athens with proof that he was King
Aigeus's son. Courtly life soon bored Theseus, so he slipped out in a storm
to tame the bull. He found shelter from the storm in the hut of an old
woman, Hekale. As in *The Victory of Berenike*, the hero's description of
the peasant's hut and their conversation takes center stage, while Callimachus deals briefly with the actual heroic exploit (killing the lion and
taming the bull). After the bull episode, Theseus returned to repay
Hekale's hospitality, but found her dead. Theseus established a deme
named after her and a shrine to Zeus Hekaleios.

The poem begins: "Once on a hill of Erekhtheos there lived an Attic
woman [Hekale] . . ." Since Erekhtheos and Erikhthonios are considered
one in some stories, that may provide the connection between the bulk of
the poem and the story of Erikhthonios's birth as told by an old crow to a
young crow toward the end of the poem. Athena wished to rear Erikhthonios, son of Hephaistos, in secret. She locked him in a chest with two
snakes and gave it to the daughters of Kekrops with orders not to open it.
When the daughters disobeyed, a crow reported this to Athena, who pun-
ished crows for bringing bad news by banishing them from the Acropolis.

After the first break in the text, the crow is the speaker until the last
eight lines.

2   They: The countryfolk of the plain of Marathon.
10 IĔ PAIEON: A cry of joy.
19 Kekrops: The mythical first king of Athens. By Aglauros he had
    three daughters—Pandrosos, Herse, and Aglauros II. During his
    reign, Athena and Poseidon contested for Attika.
23 Pallas: Another name for Athena.
26 Akhaia: The northern district of the Peloponnese.
34 spurned: Literally, "spit out."
38 eighth generation: Crows were thought to have a lifespan of ten
    human generations.
45 the Thriai: The three nymphs who taught divination. They in-
    spired the crow to prophesy about a future time when Apollo
    would change crows from white to black in punishment for
    bringing him the bad news of his lover Koronis.
48–49 A proverb.
57 The old crow fell asleep.

Lyrics

Callimachus placed four lyric poems between the *Iambi* and the *Hekale* in
his collected works; we do not know how long the lyric poems were.

For fragment 226 Pfeiffer, only the first line remains: "Ancient Lemnos, if ever another . . ." The *Diegesis* summarizes the poem: "Callimachus addresses handsome boys. Lemnos, happy in the past, became un-
happy when the women assaulted the men. So you [boys], too, should not
neglect the future." This summary refers to the myth that the women of
Lemnos neglected Aphrodite, who in revenge made them stink. Their hus-
bands turned for love to boys instead, so the women murdered all the men
on the island and lived as a community of women.

BRANKHOS Source: Fr. 229 Pfeiffer. Apollo came to his beloved
Brankhos in Didyma, an oracular center near Miletos in Asia Minor.
Brankhos descended from Apollo on his mother's side and from a priest of
Apollo on his father's side. Apollo called Brankhos from the life of a shep-
herd in order to receive Apollo's gift of prophecy.
16 double fountain: The etymology of *Didyma.*
18 Delphinios: Another name for Apollo; it means "dolphin."
19 Oikos: Another name for Miletos.

THE DEIFICATION OF ARSINOË Source: Fr. 228 Pfeiffer.
Arsinoë, sister and wife of Ptolemy II Philadelphos of Egypt, died on July 9,
270 B.C.E.; the poem was written soon after. An altar and precinct were set
up in her honor near the Emporium, the harbor area of Alexandria. The
queen's younger sister, Philotera, died before Arsinoë and was deified.
Kharis, a friend of Philotera, sees the smoke rise from Egypt and tells

Philotera that it is from Arsinoë's pyre. In the first line, "the god" is Apollo and "them" refers to the Muses.

5   Wagon: The constellation Ursa Major.

6   stolen: Arsinoë was stolen by the Dioscuri, twin brothers who were immortalized as stars.

12 noble husband: Ptolemy II Philadelphos.

14 slender: *Leptos* in Greek.

15 altar of Thetis: Located on Pharos, an island near Alexandria.

16 Thebes: The Egyptian Thebes.

28 Proteus: A sea god who lived on the island of Pharos.

32 Enna: A town in Sicily that had a temple of Demeter.

33 Lemnos: A volcanic island in the northern Aegean that was sacred to Hephaistos.

34 Deo: Another name for Demeter.

35 God-stolen: Arsinoë.

36 Kharis: The wife of Hephaistos.

52 Lame-Foot: An epithet of Hephaistos.

THE ALL-NIGHT FESTIVAL   Source: Fr. 227 Pfeiffer.

2   Erotes: Plural of *Eros*, god of love and desire.

5   kottabos: A Sicilian game with many variations; see *Akontios and Kydippe*, fragment 69, for one of them.

7   Kastor and Polydeukes, called the Dioscuri, were sons of Tyndareus and Leda. The last two lines can be reconstructed to read: "O Kastor, and you, Polydeukes, / horse-tamers, protectors of the homeless, and escorts of guests."

Milton Keynes UK
Ingram Content Group UK Ltd.
UKHW012018121023
430485UK00001B/135